DREAMSTONES

MAGIC FROM THE LIVING EARTH

RHEA LOADER

PRISM · UNITY

DREAMSTONES

Magic from the Living Earth

Published in Great Britain in 1990 by:
PRISM PRESS,
2 South Street,
Bridport,
Dorset DT6 3NQ

and distributed in the USA by:
AVERY PUBLISHING GROUP INC.,
120 Old Broadway,
Garden City Park,
New York, 11040

and published in Australia 1990 by:
UNITY PRESS,
6a Ortona Road,
Lindfield,
NSW 2070

ISBN 1 85327 054 7

Printed and bound in the Channel Islands
by The Guernsey Press Limited.

Acknowledgements

This book was created with the encouragement and assistance of some very special people in my life — Colin, who asked of me an oath; Christopher Scott, a brother who walks in magic; Bill Beattie, a beloved companion whose skilful editing added polish to the Dreamstones; Orchard Collie, helpmate and rescuer — for design, conceptual assistance and graphic critique; and Nevill Drury, who believed in the book and offered encouragement when it was most needed.

Much appreciation also to Tracie Forsyth, who collaborated on the mandala designs at beginnings of chapters; and to Amanda Radziwon, for eleventh-hour indexing.

Heartfelt thanks to Don for his courage and celebration of life, and for talking me into writing the first words of the journey; and to the women of craft who have supported, bullied, created and worked with, laughed at, celebrated and challenged me.

Dedication

If a book could be said to have a midwife, then Brandy Williams is that person; if a Muse can inhabit a sister and friend, then she is that Muse.

Contents

Part I
MAGIC FROM THE
LIVING EARTH

Chapter 1
INTRODUCTION: ANCIENT ORACLES

Divination is a way of having a dialogue with Deity, in whichever form you apprehend the mystery of the Divine. It is a way of knowing, of consulting ancient Oracles in order to perceive the patterns in the universe. Divination has many forms, ranging from the interpretation of flickering forms in the fire to the precision and order of astrology. Among the most ancient of Oracles are nature divination and stonecasting of various kinds, together with runic (secret symbol) systems and scrying (crystal gazing). Many systems contain one or more of the following elements:

1 Interpreting patterns in nature (including methods of scrying).

2 Interpreting names, numbers, planetary aspects and dreams.

3 Casting objects to form random patterns (stones, I Ching, etc.).

4 Deliberate placement of randomly chosen objects in a particular order (Tarot is a good example of this).

5 Body interpretation (hands, eyes, head, body language, etc.).

Each divinatory system is whole and complete in itself, though many diviners will use more than one system when providing an interpretation of the Oracle.

WHAT IS THE ORACLE?

The nature of the Oracle can best be explained with reference to the concept of a collective mystery, a mythic consciousness of an entire people who are part of the dreaming of the Earth Spirit, Gaea. We are all capable of contacting the Oracle, and

3

indeed do so on a nightly basis in our dreams. We are able to learn from this dreaming and take its information away with us into the everyday world, once we have learned to cultivate an attitude of acceptance of the mystery itself (which is quite beyond words, absolute meanings or concrete definitions). Our ancestors drew on this same deep well of knowledge when they consulted ancient diviners. Oracle was a term which was both the name for the mystery and, in some times and places, the name for the diviner who interpreted that mystery. Others who are attuned to that energy are poets, musicians, artists and priests, the creators of celebration and worship; these too have always been inspired by the place of collective dreaming. The Oracle is there for all who choose to listen and to create a still place within themselves wherein images from their inner awareness may be reflected.

ELEMENTS OF DIVINATION

All divinatory systems have certain elements in common:

☆ Randomising
☆ A set of Key Associations for the system
☆ Interpretation of the Keys
☆ A meaningful pattern — creating the story-line

Randomising

The wind sweeps the cloud formations across the sky, wood burns irregularly, and the waves of the ocean break in a random fashion — these and other patterns can be interpreted by a nature diviner, just as the shaking of stones or bones, the shuffle of Tarot cards or the swirl of tea-leaves randomises other systems of divination. The random element is necessary as it makes a connection between the querent (the person consulting the Oracle), the diviner and the mystery. In Tarot, cards are shuffled while the querent concentrates on the questions they have; with the I Ching, coins or yarrow sticks are shaken, then thrown; and with the Dreamstones, the stones are poured from hand to hand before being cast. The querent and diviner make a connection with their tools of divination and, through a randomising action, introduce the variables which will shape the reading.

A Set of Keys

Each system of divination has certain Keys which unlock the doors of perception, enabling the diviner to work within a specific framework. This set of associations, of meanings for particular objects, provides the basis for apprehending the pattern of energies at any given moment. Some examples of these are:

DREAMSTONES:	Twenty-three stones with assigned meanings for each stone.
SEA-STONES:	Ten stones with pictographs.
TAROT:	Seventy-eight pictorial cards (twenty-two major/fifty-six minor).
I CHING:	Eight three-line patterns called trigrams (sixty-four hexagrams).
RUNES:	Twenty-four wooden or stone tiles (sometimes with one blank) with linear symbols inscribed.
NUMEROLOGY:	Nine numbers, each with assigned meaning.
PALMISTRY:	Major lines on hand have (astrologically related) Key meanings; shape changes from person to person.
ASTROLOGY:	Configuration of heavens at time of birth is translated into two-dimensional pattern; this is broken down into meanings for Planets, the area of the sky they fall in (Astrological Signs), and the numbering of

that quadrant in relation to
the horizon (Houses).

These Keys also relate to systems of magic, religious worship
and mystery traditions, so there are deeper meanings available
to those who choose to meditate on the Keys. In a divinatory
setting, knowledge of the more esoteric aspects of these Keys
enhances the psychic skills of the diviner, enabling them to call
on a wealth of ancient wisdom in the practice of their Art.

Interpretation of the Keys

The Keys are interpreted within a specific framework and in a
particular order. In the ancient forms of nature divination,
there are traditional meanings for wind blowing from different
directions, the groupings and directions of movement of birds,
cattle, fish and wild game. These meanings are often particular
to the people of a specific region and will clearly reflect the way
of life and belief structures of that people. If someone from a
different culture is to learn that people's system of divination,
then it is necessary to understand the framework which gives it
validity; changes can then be made to the system in a
meaningful manner to reflect personal reality. In systems
which post-date hunter/gatherer societies, and specifically in
those systems which are utilised in a modern context, an
understanding of the original framework is essential. If we are
isolated from a sense of history and tradition, then there is little
comprehension of the depth and subtlety of ancient devices. In
learning about Norse runes, for example, it is necessary to
understand their original cultural context, so that modern
meanings can be attributed to the Keys. An example here is
their 'F' rune, which is traditionally associated with cattle, and
therefore, to the original Nordic diviners, wealth. In modern
terms, we could justifiably associate this rune with liquid
assets, stocks and bonds, wealth which can easily be traded for
other goods or services. This rune has a number of more
esoteric meanings, which may similarly be translated in this
fashion.

A Meaningful Pattern

To be useful to a reader, a personally meaningful interpretation of the pattern must be discovered. This is the element which separates book learning from the true art of divination, and is perhaps the most complicated to master. A story-line is created from the combination of individual Keys and the applied psychic skills of the diviner in consultation with the Oracle.

CREATING A SYSTEM

This book explores a system of stonecasting which has its origins in the mythic systems and divinatory practices of a number of ancient peoples. The Dreamstone system draws on Celtic, Pictish and Saxon traditions, which have then been synthesised with more primitive systems which continue to be used by indigenous peoples around the world.

It has always been important to me that divination reach for the deepest connection with the Earth, with mystery traditions and ancient knowledge, in order to have the ability to re-link the individual with a sense of history and purpose. If there is no sense of where we are coming from, of our personal past and context in society, then it is very difficult to make decisions on direction for the future. Divination allows you to interpret the patterns around you in the light of self-knowledge and inner awareness; this in turn provides a framework for interpretation of the mysteries of the Oracle.

In primitive societies, the social dynamics were governed by sophisticated patterns of behaviour and expectations based on the individuals having a particular place in that society. Mental and emotional disorders were the province of the shaman or priest who would interpret or divine the will of the Gods, using lots — stones, bones or other devices — as a focus for their questions. These mystics would, in ritual fashion, introduce a random element into the process of divination by shaking bones together, tumbling them onto the ground, or asking their querent to select a few objects from a selection of many. Placing these objects in a deliberate arrangement, or casting them to form a random pattern, would provide the basis for the reading. The diviner, after preparing themselves carefully, would look at the pattern, then at the individual elements in that pattern, for the information which they could interpret. A story would be created from the placement of the objects, the relationship between them and the overall pattern of the querent's life, placing the information in a context which would have meaning.

With the Dreamstones, I have drawn from these elements of traditional divination to create a system of stonecasting which allows you to interpret the patterns in your own life, and other people's lives, in an intuitive but very practical fashion. In working with the Dreamstones, we start by reaching for the deepest and most personal areas of concern to humankind throughout history — Earth (the body, food and shelter), Water (fluids, emotions, relating), Fire (warmth, energy, sexuality), and Air (breath, mind and communication). We travel from there into an exploration of Planetary energies and other metaphysical factors, each assigned to a different stone. The Keys for these areas are interpreted for each individual by taking into account the placement of the stones, the relationship of meanings and the context in which the interpretation is being offered. The 'Magic from the Living Earth' is the power of the stones to connect you with Earth energies, and the power of transformation which comes from your intuitive or psychic ability and self knowledge.

WHO SEEKS DIVINATION?

Almost everyone seeks to divine, for themselves, what *will* happen next, and also seeks to make sense of what *has* happened and what *is* happening in the world around them. Divination, or fascination with it, is one of the essential elements of the human psyche.

Some people choose to enhance and train this ability and may, like a talented musician, artist or poet, have a real gift for it; others will work with divination to become quite competent interpreters of the patterns in their own life, but may not choose to interpret those patterns for others.

Chapter 2
HOW TO USE THIS BOOK

The book is divided into regular chapters with subheadings. However, the following diagram divides the process of working with the book into five stages — Novice, Apprentice, Traveller, Magister and Teacher. These stages are a symbolic journey through the elements which will lead to the almost inevitable changes you will make to the system once you have made it your own.

NOVICE

This stage is ruled by Earth as it represents the foundation and history of the system.

1   Read the introductory chapters up to the end of the section on 'Dreams and Omens' in Chapter 4, *Dreams and Stones*. Start to work with a Dream Journal so that you become familiar with the process of interpreting the messages of the Oracle which filter through your Dreaming Self.

2   Continue through the material in *Dreams and Stones* which explores the connection between interpretation of dreams and interpretation of divinatory devices. An example is given of a page for recording and exploring your dreams.

3   Chapter 5, *Beginning Divination*, concentrates on one of the oldest, and simplest, methods of lithomancy (stonecasting) and its ability to provide basic information — the Yes/No/Question stones. Begin to work with this method and record your results.

APPRENTICE

This stage is ruled by Water, associated with trusting your

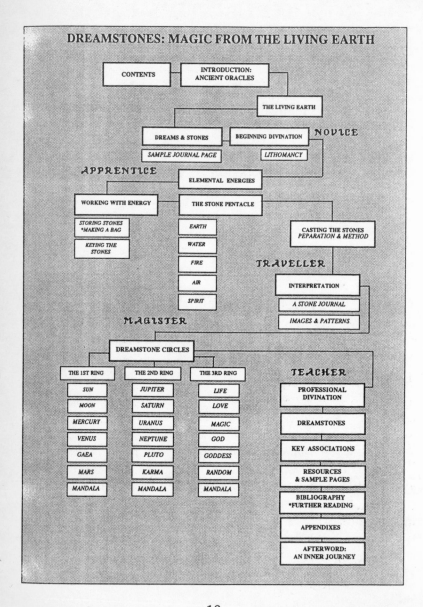

DREAMSTONES: MAGIC FROM THE LIVING EARTH

CONTENTS

INTRODUCTION: ANCIENT ORACLES

THE LIVING EARTH

DREAMS & STONES

BEGINNING DIVINATION

NOVICE

SAMPLE JOURNAL PAGE

LITHOMANCY

APPRENTICE

ELEMENTAL ENERGIES

WORKING WITH ENERGY

THE STONE PENTACLE

STORING STONES
*MAKING A BAG

EARTH

KEYING THE STONES

WATER

CASTING THE STONES
PEPARATION & METHOD

FIRE

AIR

TRAVELLER

SPIRIT

INTERPRETATION

A STONE JOURNAL

MAGISTER

IMAGES & PATTERNS

DREAMSTONE CIRCLES

THE 1ST RING	THE 2ND RING	THE 3RD RING	TEACHER
SUN	JUPITER	LIFE	PROFESSIONAL DIVINATION
MOON	SATURN	LOVE	
MERCURY	URANUS	MAGIC	DREAMSTONES
VENUS	NEPTUNE	GOD	
GAEA	PLUTO	GODDESS	KEY ASSOCIATIONS
MARS	KARMA	RANDOM	RESOURCES & SAMPLE PAGES
MANDALA	MANDALA	MANDALA	BIBLIOGRAPHY *FURTHER READING

APPENDIXES

AFTERWORD: AN INNER JOURNEY

feelings and the power of your dreams. You have begun to cast the stones and have taken the first steps in the divinatory process.

1 Read through Chapter 6, *Elemental Energies*, which also relates to the stages of learning the Dreamstones.

2 *Working with Energy*, Chapter 7, focuses on the storage, protection and energising of your stones; all part of the ongoing care which we give to any magical tool in exchange for the gifts it returns to us.

3 Start at the beginning of the *Stone Pentacle*, Chapter 8, and work through each section in turn. DO THE EXERCISES. If you skimp on the exercises, then you are probably avoiding something, namely the necessity to look deeply at yourself before attempting to interpret energies or events in your own life or the lives of others. Self-knowledge is important to a diviner; it is also a responsibility which is owed to the people who will seek your aid. It is reasonable to expect that you will work at your Art, and interpret the patterns in another person's life in a harmonious and balanced fashion. This harmony is based on knowledge of the self.

4 *Casting the Stones*, Chapter 9, concentrates on centring and personal preparation before a stonecasting, together with information on methods for creating a pattern for interpretation.

TRAVELLER

This stage is ruled by Fire, associated with enthusiasm for adventures and the energy to explore new possibilities. The Traveller has chosen stones, worked with the aspects of their personality which correspond to those stones, and energised them for divination.

1 *Interpreting the Oracle* is discussed in Chapter 10, together with patterns which will arise, groups of stones and symbolic images. When you are familiar with these patterns, you may want to cast the stones for another person; methods are explored and ways of recording stonecasting are discussed. Two sample interpretations of the Stone Pentacle casting are examined at this stage.

2 You should now concentrate on casting the stones for yourself on a regular basis, recording the information in your journal. Note particular information which is emphasised both in your dreams and in divination. Practise casting the stones for friends.

MAGISTER

This next section is ruled by Air, as there are more decisions to be made about different stones, and concentration on learning the system. For daily stonecasting and simple interpretations, you can cast the Stone Pentacle or the Yes/No/Question stones. However, for more information and deeper understanding of a situation or facet of your psyche, the Three Rings are invaluable.

1 Read the material on *Dreamstone Circles*, Chapter 11, and skim through the *Three Rings*. Go back to the beginning of the First Ring and start to work with each stone in turn, reading the commentary and relying on your own dreams and personal knowledge of what the stones mean to you. At the end of the First Ring, there is a ritual for joining these stones with those of the *Stone Pentacle*. You will then be able to interpret the subtleties of divination in a more complete manner.

2 Work through the Second Ring and Third Ring in the same way, stopping at the end of each Ring to integrate the stones with those of preceding sets.

3 Work with the full set of the Dreamstones until you have acquired facility with their interpretation.

TEACHER

This last stage corresponds with Spirit, where you have integrated the four elements into one whole. Your own reading and the practice of divination will probably lead to changes being made in the system — a stone added, another substituted. Everyone who has worked with the system has made some changes to it to reflect the changes in their own personality over time, or to explore an aspect of their character which seems to need its own stone. In turn, you too will teach others

your variations — these variations are also Dreamstones;
stones of your own dreaming, containing the magic from the
living Earth.

1 Chapter 12, *Professional Divination*, concentrates on the step
of becoming a professional Diviner (should you so decide), and
includes discussion of the kinds of people who are likely to
come to you for Divination. This Chapter also includes
guidelines and advice about counselling.

2 In Chapter 13, *Dreamstones* is about variations to the system,
giving examples of extra stones and changes that have been
made by different people.

3 *Key Associations* is a section dedicated to the magic of
similarities — the colours, plants, and some esoteric correspondences for each stone in the Dreamstones are listed for easy
reference.

4 *Resources and Sample Pages* include blank templates for a
Dream Journal and Stone Journal, together with a partial guide
to lapidary and supply shops for stones.

5 *Appendices* provide additional information relating to the
Dreamstones, including another allied system of stonecasting,
and an afterword on the author's journey into stonecasting and
divination.

Chapter 3
THE LIVING EARTH

> Tumble the bones and cast the lots of time, hear the
> fall of stones, echoing in a silent place, woven by the
> fates.   *Rhea Loader 1988*

The concept of the Earth as a living organism is not limited to
spiritual perception; it is an idea which an increasing number
of mainstream scientists are beginning to explore. In the late
1960s and early 1970s photographs appeared in magazines and
on television screens, in newspapers and on posters around the
world, showing the image of the Earth from space — an image
now familiar to all of us. It is probably not surprising that this
led to a new perception of the Earth as a whole, and sparked a
revision of belief structures and cultural assumptions.

A number of different people independently articulated
(first in print by Tim Zell) a concept which is usually attributed
to Dr James Lovelock, a noted British ecologist. This concept,
an eco-evolutionary theory, came to be called the Gaea
Hypothesis, named for the ancient Greek Earth Goddess, Gaea.
This postulated, amongst its arguments, an indivisible link
between the eco-system and the biosphere.

It is no longer possible to disconnect our individual lives
from the needs of the natural environment. A reconnection
with natural cycles is now being made by many people, and
often this prompts a re-examination of past cultures which
stressed the necessity of this connection. One such is the
culture of Ancient Greece, and the classical mythos which is its
foundation.

In pre-Homeric Greece, the Earth is known as Gaea, a
Goddess, but one without anthropomorphic form. Later,
aspects of the Earth Goddess such as Demeter (patroness of
agriculture), Persephone (daughter of Demeter and ruler of the

Underworld — mother of Dionysus), and Pandora (the first human woman) are worshipped; however, it is in her original form of the Earth itself that we find Her inspiring.

This concept of the Earth as a living entity is central to working with the Dreamstones. Gaea is essentially important in that it was her serpent which gave the power of divination at Delphi (a place renowned for sacred connection with the Earth and with the Oracle). Later, Apollo subsumed the power of the serpent and it was his priestesses who interpreted the Oracle. The Oracle itself, which harkens back to prehistory, remained intact; only the outer forms of divination changed.

BONES OF THE EARTH

One of the oldest and most valuable of Earth's gifts comes from within Her body and is part of Her form and structure — stones for building, tools, making fire (flint and iron pyrite), for art, decoration, ochres for dyes, for recording ideas and impressions.

Making and interpreting patterns with stone is a practice that goes back to Neolithic times. There are stone circles, spirals and burial cairns scattered across Europe, Britain and Ireland. The stones were aligned with the movement of the heavens, with precise measurements marking the passage of the days and seasons, Solstices, Equinoxes and lunar cycles. This use of stone is an example of how our species recognises patterns in nature and creates a symbolic system to record those observations.

It was not just the placement of stones, however, which gave them meaning. The energy created by the deliberate gathering of the right stones, and arrangement of them in a particular way, was also important. Our ancestors related to places on an individual basis and recognised that each tree and rock, river and plant had its own spirit. As spirituality came to be more separated from place, abstractions became more commonplace and awareness of power residing in particular locations faded. William Blake, in *The Marriage of Heaven and Hell*, referred to this phenomenon:

> The ancient Poets animated all sensible objects with
> Gods or Geniuses, calling them by the names and
> adorning them with the properties of woods, rivers,

mountains, lakes, cities, nations, and whatever their enlarged and numerous senses could perceive . . .

With stonecasting, we may reconcile our estrangement from the land and enlarge our senses to perceive more of the living Earth. We do this by working with Her bones, the stones themselves, and anchoring our psyche with their energies. The stones have their own individuality, feeling and identity, and by examining natural rhythms, places and cycles, and the properties of stones, we can dream these energies into our own lives.

MAKING CONNECTIONS

Have you ever carried a round pebble in your pocket as a worry stone — a stone that made you feel balanced, secure and comforted? Then you have already made a connection with stone as an energy conductor and symbol for ideas. The worry stone is smooth and regular in shape, cool to the touch at first, but quickly warmed by your hand. Its familiarity is comforting as it builds up mental associations over a period of time. A pleasant habit sometimes develops, of holding it in times of stress, worry or tension.

Have you ever gathered coloured pebbles on a beach, or stones with interesting patterns? Fossicked for semi-precious stones or crystals whilst on vacation? Then you are already attracted to stones and appreciate them as an aesthetic representation of Earth's art. The coloured pebbles can be sorted into stones which seem, to you, to have different vibrations or feelings to them. The range extends from those stones which feel calm and relaxing to those which feel energetic and vibrant.

Quiet Stones

Quiet, calm stones are good to carry with you when you are feeling tense or worried. They can be placed in bowls around the house to ensure that a tranquil environment is maintained. Relaxing stones make very good worry stones and are usually smooth and rounded, their smoothness being symbolic of quiet and harmony.

Energetic Stones

These can be carried around with you to add a boost of energy, especially when you are feeling tired or are required to expend a large quantity of energy. They can be placed in a bowl in a work-room or exercise place to ensure that enthusiasm does not flag.

Healing Stones

These are traditionally such stones as amethyst (which cleanses all that it comes into contact with, hence its association as a poison curative), jade (which is associated with the release of tension or cure of fevers), and carnelian or bloodstone (which is associated with cure of blood disorders, excessive bleeding or viruses). Other stones which are associated with healing are quartz (for clarity of thought), lapis lazuli (freedom from possession, protection from disease) and ruby (for general good health and vitality). There are many books on the subject of gems and healing (see *Bibliography*); the most useful stone I have found for general healing is amethyst. It releases blockages in your aura and promotes both clarity of thinking and spiritual openness, discouraging bigotry or a closed mind. It is useful to carry a healing stone around with you in a pocket, or as a pendant around your neck, as this prevents your picking up negativity from your surroundings.

Anger Stones

Stones which release the power of anger are traditionally dark in colour, such as obsidian, granite, jet and black river-stones. Because the black absorbs all light, it is thought that it also absorbs all dark emotions. A process of releasing anger is to concentrate it into a black stone over a period of time (say from full moon to dark moon — a period of two weeks) and then throw the stone into the sea to be cleansed. An alternative is to work with feelings of anger on a daily basis and surround the stone with salt to ward the negativity from you; at the end of each session, place the stone in a cup of heavily salted water; after a set period of time, say again two weeks, pour the salt water down the drain where it will find its own way to the sea.

17

The stone, once rinsed in salt water and then pure water, is ready to be used again. A caution here: this technique will work only on anger left over from past events. The best way to deal with anger in the present is to take positive action, to deal with the situation in a direct manner. Exhaust the alternatives first, and then if you must deal with a situation which you feel cannot be altered, you can at least deal with your own anger about it in a positive way.

CHOOSING SIZE OF STONES

When you are choosing a stone for a particular purpose, keep in mind the colour which represents that purpose to you, and what shape and size you would like the stone to be.

Dreamstones

The Dreamstones should be the size of your thumb-nail and round, so that they scatter well. Tumbled, polished stones are the best as they capture and reflect light, and these are freely available, at a modest price, at most lapidary supply shops. The full set of Dreamstones is over twenty in number, so large stones will not all fit in the palm of one hand. The number of stones you wish to cast in your set will govern the size required.

PURCHASE OF STONES

Either from your local gemstore or lapidary shop, or special sets can be ordered from:
Dreamstones, GPO Box 1030, Canberra, ACT 2601, Australia.
'Mythos', PO Box 21768, Seattle, Wa. 98111-3768, USA.
'Mysteries', 9-11 Monmouth Street, Covent Garden, London WC2H 9DA, England.

Special orders are taken on number of stones, colour and size. These are all presented in pouches which protect the stones and will be chosen by the author and other Dreamstone diviners.

A PERSONAL CHOICE

The stones which I recommend in this book for each Element, Planet and aspect of life, are my personal preferences. You will, necessarily, be different, so choose stones which suit you. An example of this individualising process is my choice of stone attributed to the Planet Venus. The associations given by traditional books on correspondences tell me that this stone should be coloured green. However, I see Venus as a deep crimson stone with a smooth texture (my own stone is a red tiger's-eye), symbolising the harmony and sensuality of that planetary sphere. At all times you must be guided by your own inner sense of what stone will be right for you.

In divination there are never absolutes, only interpretations; this applies as much to tools you choose to work with (in this case, stones) as to your own life and personal feelings.

Stones as Gifts

In ancient times, the Persians and Greeks gave each other egg-shaped stones to mark the beginning of spring. These semi-precious stones represented the cycle of renewal, and new beginnings. In giving a gemstone egg they were saying 'I give you this gift to renew our friendship, to signify that it will be as strong as this stone, and as beautiful.'

I hope your experience with the Dreamstones will be the beginning of a journey into strength, beauty and connection with the Earth.

Chapter 4
DREAMS AND STONES

Why are dreams important? Historically, dreams have been relied upon in prophecy and divination as they were thought to be messages from the Gods. In modern times, psychologists (both Freudian and Jungian) make their own studies of the importance of dreams, seeing them, variously, as a sorting process to make sense of the day's events or a communication between different parts of the psyche. In Jungian analysis, the symbols in dreams are associated with archetypal images, broken down into their component parts, and examined in order to understand their significance. Dreams are explored for their meaning and for what the symbolism within them indicates about our thinking processes. I take a view which combines aspects of the ancient understanding with that of modern practice: that dreams are the voice of the Divine speaking through the Oracle into our sleeping minds; that they are a sorting process which creates systems and patterns; that their images and symbolism, when explored, provide both divinatory information and a key to self-knowledge.

Each person is able to make contact with the Oracle, with the personal answers that are found deep inside our own being. Many have cut themselves away from that knowledge by ignorance, deliberate denial and social custom. However, as becomes apparent in analysis, even people who have not consciously remembered dreams in years, start to remember once they are given permission to do so by an 'expert'. In the world of inner space, each person is their own master or mistress, so permission to listen to the voice of inner knowledge must come from within.

Dreaming is one of the ways of undertaking a dialogue with your inner self, with that part of your being which comprehends the messages and the mythic reality of the Oracle. If we

20

imagine the Oracle as a deep still pool of water or a primal sea of consciousness, of collective thoughts, feelings and knowledge, our dreams can be seen as glimmerings of light reflected on its surface. The images we bring back from dreams enlarge our perceptions, and enable us to derive meaning from our relationship with the Oracle. In turn, these images sensitise us to the patterns and images in nature. This allows us to interpret omens and portents in the everyday world by applying the skills of dream interpretation to them.

OMENS

Omens arise spontaneously, without our looking for them, whereas in systems of divination and scrying there is a deliberate process of training which triggers our psychic vision. Omens appear in dreams and give us information (often cloaked in metaphor) about events which are likely to happen in the external world. Premonitions of danger, success, births and deaths are the most common, probably because they are things that affect us in a deeply emotional manner. One such omen will be familiar to you from one version of the Arthurian tale: a dream that a dragon would be seen in the sky and that this would be a sign that a King of all Albion would appear to unite the people. This related to a comet appearing at a significant historical time (an image which could be associated with a fiery dragon in the mind's eye). The interpretation was a symbolic one, though the event it related to was something physical, and obvious at the time of its occurrence. It is often the case with omens that the event to which they relate is not made clear until the time of its happening, and this makes the interpretation of omens a particularly uncertain way of divining the future.

In our own dreaming, a death vision may relate to physical death, but more often it will be a symbolic vision indicating a painful ending — of a relationship, a belief system or a way of life. Premonitions of danger can prompt us to take more care and pay attention to what we are doing, thereby eliminating or minimising the threat. Perhaps if some of these stronger warnings were acknowledged, the happenings would not take place. This faculty is particularly useful when you are planning

21

a long-distance journey, especially where your safety depends on the concentration of another person; for example, a bus driver or aeroplane pilot. It is quite common to hear reports after a major disaster (an aeroplane crash, for example, or a ship sinking — as happened with the *Titanic*) that confirm late cancellations of tickets by people who had a premonition of danger associated with their intended voyage. You will learn to gauge more clearly which visions relate to physical events, and interpret those which are more purely symbolic in the appropriate manner. In many cases, however, forewarned is truly forearmed, and knowledge of an event can sometimes prevent the worst aspects from manifesting.

A personal example of this was a dream about a robbery, followed by a real feeling of foreboding when I returned home the next day. There was nothing out of place, yet I awoke the next morning with an even stronger feeling of imminent danger. It was so uncomfortable that I felt almost ill, and stayed home that day from work. Halfway through the day, there was a knock on the door which I ignored at first. When I went to the door, there was a man there who was very surprised to find someone home; he spun me a fake-sounding story about looking for a person to whom he had sold a car, who had given that address — however, my dream had forewarned me. Following him out to the gate, to see that he was off the property, I took note of the licence plate of the car he was driving. He ran to the car and took off rather suddenly, further confirming my suspicions. I rang the police and reported the incident as an attempted break-in; they advised that the car was stolen and my reading of the situation was, in their view, accurate.

Unfortunately, though, omens and premonitions are not always this clear. In another incident, again relating to theft of personal property, a close friend who was to meet me on a particular day had a prophetic dream. He dreamt of a wallet being stolen, so took precautions and removed his rent money from the wallet before leaving the house. I was late in meeting him as my purse had been stolen on the way. It was the right dream image, but the interpretation related it to the wrong person.

On the whole, omens and premonitions in dreams are

22

allegorical rather than actual. It seems wise to treat these strong feelings warily and with respect unless you are absolutely certain they relate to a particular person or event. The images are most significant in making you pay attention to your surroundings in a more careful manner — the raised adrenalin of slight uneasiness makes it possible to avoid dangerous situations, or react more quickly than usual to events around you.

A DREAM JOURNAL

A dream journal is a valuable tool for examining your own inner landscape. It will give you an ongoing emotional weather report, letting you know how your feelings change from day to day and allow you to bring more information from dreams into your conscious mind. Living as we do in a technological culture, there is not much emphasis placed on the power to be found in dreams and divinatory practices on an everyday or practical basis. We have cultivated a selective inattention to this area of our life and have been isolated from a sense of connectedness and inner meaning.

Keeping a journal will gradually break down these acquired barriers and make deeper insight possible. The process of writing a daily comment, however brief, opens channels of communication to the Dreaming Self and, in turn, to the Oracle. Your 'enlarged and numerous senses' (as Blake phrased it) will focus your attention equally on both inner and outer landscapes, dreaming and waking worlds. Once you have started to pay attention to your dreams, more accurate interpretation of divinatory devices will be possible. The ability to turn an image or pattern in divination into a meaningful story is enhanced by practising on interpretation of dream scenarios and symbols.

Preparation

Purchase a blank book or ruled notebook, or photocopy the sample page which appears at the end of this book. Place your journal beside your bed with a favourite pen nearby (one that will write on an angle; remember, you will be lying down or semi-reclining when you write in your journal).

The Blank Page

One of the most difficult parts of writing a journal is overcoming the intimidation of an entirely blank page. Everyone dreams, and it is easy to overcome the tyranny of imagining you have to write brilliant prose first thing in the morning. Mornings are not the best time of day for me, so writing in a journal has to be an easy thing to do before I am willing to make the effort. This method I have found sufficiently painless to persevere with, even on my worst, sleep-befuddled days.

To remember what you have dreamt, the first step is to tell yourself that you will remember. The second step in dream memory is to be still and quiet for a few moments when you awake. Do not interrupt the end of your dreaming by moving, even to change position. Recall the dream you have just had — if you can quietly concentrate on it when you first awake, more details will be available to you. Fragments of this and other dreams are likely to spring to mind at different stages of the day, but these will not be as complete as the first waking memory. When you have the dream firmly in conscious memory you are less likely to forget the details; do not move or think of writing it down until you have replayed it in your mind's eye. Then take up pen and paper and begin to write. Sometimes you may start by writing colours you remember — a yellow raincoat, a blue sky, a red mailbox or a brown coat — and proceed to other details like 'It was raining and the wind was strong', 'A strange dream where impossible things seemed commonplace', or details of rooms or surroundings or people.

If you cannot recall your last dream, then the first thing you write is *how you feel today*. For example 'I had a great sleep and have lots of energy', or 'Lots of fragmented dreams, but no clear images', or perhaps 'Wish I could stay in bed today'. The first comment (whether it be on a dream or a feeling) messes up the blank page, and you can begin to record images and other impressions from there.

IMAGES FROM DREAMS

You might ask 'What images are the important ones?', or 'How do dream images tell me anything practical or useful?'. Everything in a dream is significant — colours, symbols, situations, people, feelings and impressions. Dreams speak to us in the language of symbolism and metaphor. We come to understand that particular images relate to our parents, our jobs, our relationships or goals in a metaphorical way. They are like roads drawn on a map — representations of reality, but not the territory itself. Like a road-map, there is no complete and fully accurate representation of the territory you will cover, but the map still gives valuable information on relative distances between places, and the importance of major routes. In dreams, there are images and metaphors for reality which appear to be more important or significant than other images in the same dream.

Recording Images

These images should be underlined when you write them down for they are a message from your Dreaming Self. On the sample page, there is a space for drawing images or representations of things which appeared in your dream landscape. Do not be worried about artistic skill — after all, no-one else will see the drawing in your private journal — but do be as creative with it as possible. Coloured pencils, scribbled biro lines, crayons and even marking pens can be used to give an impression of what you have seen in your dreams. I recall one morning when I awoke feeling distressed, angry and agitated without being able to remember very much detail from my dreams; I wrote how I felt and then used the drawing space to scribble slashes and crossed lines in dark colours and bright red. The emotions were expressed very clearly in that drawing; later I was able to recall what had triggered that emotional storm and deal with the energies in a practical way.

Write down any images you remember — not worrying about the order in which they appeared. For example, 'I remember looking at a crimson scarf, worn around the neck of a very old woman', or 'Tony was in my dream, but he didn't look right' or 'The ocean/big waves/sky/being dragged under but being able to breathe/sand/colours/danger', or perhaps 'An aeroplane, travelling overseas/not having packed properly/

running late/hurry/feeling anxious'.

As you work with dreams, you will find that it becomes easier to record impressions and to find personal significance and meaning in the images you remember. This journey into the internal landscape will make you more aware of the images from the Oracle that arise spontaneously. This, in turn, adds to your ability to interpret patterns and metaphorical symbols in different systems of divination. You will become accustomed to creating a quiet, listening space in your mind on awakening and interpreting the things you see there.

Leave space at the bottom of each page for significant patterns you observe and their interpretation. Over a couple of days you might think of other patterns which emerge, so if possible carry your journal around with you. I have lost track of the number of times I have stopped in the middle of shopping, or on a bus journey, to write new information in my journal, so can recommend the practice.

A SAMPLE JOURNAL PAGE

There is a blank version of this following page included in the 'Resources and Sample Pages' section on page 157. Please feel free to photocopy it if you would like to use this format for recording and interpreting your dreams.

DREAMS AND STONES

Once you have started to record dreams and impressions, insights into your deepest feelings start to surface. If you are working on a particular exercise, or with a particular stone, you can programme your mind to an extent by concentrating on the aspects of your character that are resonant with that stone. Dreams which relate to your deepest knowledge of that energy will then follow. In this way, your Dreaming Self and Conscious Self are linked in paying attention to each facet of your character in turn.

The importance of dreams in stimulating the intuitive process cannot be stressed enough. If we record our dreams, and then record our changing relationship with the stones which we have selected as oracular tools, we address that part of our mind which is resonant with the Oracle. Divination,

A DREAM JOURNAL

DATE   SEASON

MOON PHASE   DAY OF CYCLE

FEELINGS...

IMAGES & IDEAS

SIGNIFICANT PATTERNS & INTERPRETATIONS

PAGE #

which extends from intuition, is a function of the spirit that exists in the spaces between the senses and acts as a bridge for information from the Divine.

There are many ways of talking about this process, but whether we attribute it to the anima (the feminine within us all), the right hemisphere (holistic awareness, non-linear thought), or to religious perception, we are speaking of a way of discerning reality which is quite distinct from everyday practical perceptions. This does not mean intuition, or the world of divination, of the Oracle is any less real than chairs, morning newspapers or the ground we walk upon; it is simply a different order of reality. Dream images and intuitions on meanings of stones can be more useful to you than all the commentaries written by other people. For this reason, this book includes a commentary at the beginning of each section on the Elements, followed by exercises which link the commentary to your own perceptions; then there is space left for your own comments which will arise from intuitions, dreams and experience.

Recording Impressions

I spent a set amount of time on each stone when I was creating the Dreamstone system. You can decide for yourself whether you would like to work with each stone for three days, a week, a lunar month or some other time period. However, at least three days should be spent on each stone to realise fully the potential it contains. At later stages, you may find it necessary to do additional work on a particular stone or combination of stones in order to understand the part of your life which is affected by their energy.

In my journal notes, I can trace my changing impressions of the meanings of the stones. My early notes say of the Earth Stone that it 'relates to all things on the home front, hearth and marriage and committed relationships of all kinds — friendships, parenthood and immediate environment. It is the anchor-point of consciousness, relaxation, repose and trust. It is home . . .' Later, when I added to my stones, I separated some of these aspects into different stones — the Love, Earth and Home Stones. The Love Stone is concerned with 'relationships of the heart, with your mother, nurturing and emotional fulfilment'. The Earth Stone came to represent 'the element of earth, practicality, wisdom, wealth and the body'. The Home Stone went through its own changes and came to be called the Gaea stone. It still has some of the above attributes, but its position in a casting also tells me what a querent's relationship is with nature, Earth cycles and the natural environment.

As you can see, the journal makes note of these changes and lets you know how you have changed over a period of time. I have given exercises for the first section of the Dreamstones in *The Stone Pentacle* (Chapter 8). Record your own experiences and thoughts on each exercise, and create new ways of exploring the part of your personality which resonates with each stone.

In the latter part of the book, I describe the Three Rings, which comprise my own relationship with the Dreamstones; other people to whom I have introduced the system have made very different relationships with the Oracle and chosen very different stones and meanings. I would like to encourage you to explore the Three Rings in your own dreams, keeping the same kind of notes you made for the Stone Pentacle, then validating your intuitions by your own life experiences and relationship with that part of your psyche. Adding one stone at a time to the set of Dreamstones allows you to integrate the new meanings and combinations, and deepens your ability to interpret the Oracle.

Part II
PRACTICAL STONE MAGIC

Chapter 5
BEGINNING DIVINATION

A diviner begins with the simplest forms of divination and proceeds from there to wherever his interest and skill leads. Symbols (cards, stones, runes, etc.) are either cast randomly or arranged in a particular pattern. One of the easiest skills to acquire is that of stonecasting, for it depends on relationship of objects rather than remembering set placements for the stones. It is also a direct way of making a connection with the natural forces of the Earth, for the stones have their own individual connection with those energies. The following method will only give you answers for 'yes', 'no' or 'maybe'. Its simplicity is deceptive since the number of questions you can ask is limited only by your own imagination.

A caution here — ask only three questions in any one session and relate them to a particular event, and *never* ask a question to which you do not really want to know the answer. If a 'no' will dismay you, then perhaps the question is not appropriate; similarly, a 'yes' may also prove to be alarming. Emotional issues 'does s/he love me?' are not considered appropriate because you are not able to be dispassionate about the outcome and will influence the fall of stones accordingly.

PREPARATION

Gather three stones to represent Yes, No and the Question. They can be any colour you like and need only represent the above three qualities to you personally. Many diviners choose a light stone for Yes, a dark one for No, and a bright coloured stone (red, blue or green, for example) for the Question. The stones can be ones that you find in the garden or near the seaside, or semi-precious tumbled stones from a gem shop. Keep an open mind to possibilities and you will find your own stones fairly quickly. A variation on stones is to use coloured sea shells; however, they are more fragile and not inclined to last as long — a disadvantage in the long term — but are otherwise acceptable, especially if you are impatient to begin divination immediately.

METHOD

☆ Find an uninterrupted place and sit comfortably on the ground.

☆ Take three deep breaths to centre your energy.

☆ Hold the three stones clasped between your hands and clearly think of your question.

☆ Tumble the stones in your hands to imprint them with your energy.

☆ When you are ready, cast the stones onto the ground.

INTERPRETATION

☆ The stone closest to the Question Stone is your answer.

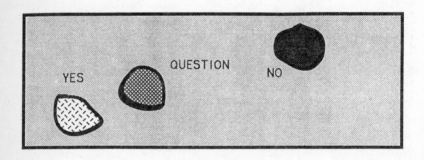

☆ If both stones are equally close, or nearly so, then the answer is uncertain. You may read this as 'undecided' or 'maybe'.

34

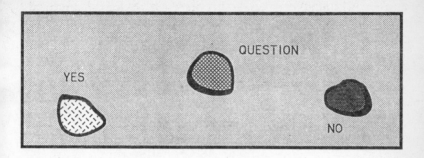

TIMING

The above method can also be used to give information on Past, or Future. The Yes Stone represents the Future, the No Stone the Past (or memories) and the Question Stone is the Present. If you ask whether an event will occur in one casting and receive a 'yes', then you could cast the stones again to determine whether the answer relates to a past or future event. Again, the stone which is closest to the Question Stone provides the answer.

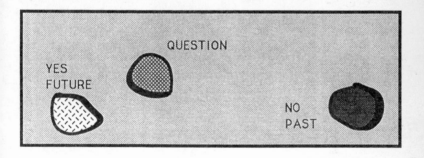

☆ If both stones are equal distance from the Question Stone, then you can assume that the answer is relevant for the present.

CONTINUING DIVINATION

The first steps of reading relationships between stones now lead into more complex patterns. In divination, a reading does not only concentrate on the positive or negative aspects of a pattern. A stonecasting makes a composite of these and places them in perspective. This means working with stones which represent your relationship with the world around you.

While there are no absolute certainties for combinations of stones, the exercises in this book enable you to make connections which are personally meaningful. Your reading will be dependent on your skill, experience, and random factors at the time of the stonecasting. The Art of Divination is a journey into self-knowledge and changed perceptions. You will in turn assist others to see clearly the events which surround them.

YES	NO	QUESTION
POSITIVE	NEGATIVE	THE ISSUE
THE FUTURE	THE PAST	THE PRESENT

Chapter 6
ELEMENTAL ENERGIES

The energies which combine in the world have qualities which we can recognise in all living things. We perceive reality as a combination of material and spiritual, an interweaving of energy and matter, force and form.

Our remote ancestors' lives were governed by elemental forces; by wind, fire, rain and ice, and by the need to find shelter, warmth, food and companionship. They, too, looked at the spiritual side of life and explained their world in terms of the spirits which governed the elemental forces. Much later, some philosophers divided the world into the elements of Air, Fire, Water and Earth; with the fifth vibration, Spirit, being a synergy of the other four, that which exists beyond the material or concrete in the world. These elemental principles were symbols which described the complex interrelationship between force and form and came to have many applications in esoteric studies. In Western esoteric lore, ideas and intuitions regarding these principles came to be accepted and a general body of information about their relationships was created.

Air can be associated with the wind; with dawn, new beginnings and the season of spring. In human life, Air is the first breath which heralds the separation from the womb, and other correspondences are consciousness, waking, activity and thought. *Fire* can be associated with lightning; with noon, exploration, spontaneous happenings, creativity and the season of summer. In human life, Fire is the awakening of sexuality with puberty. Other correspondences are life, force, will and extremes of behaviour. *Water* came to be associated with rain and flood; with twilight, reflection on events, imagination and the season of autumn. In human life, Water is the time of maturity, of moving away from the concerns of childhood. Other correspondences are night, dreams, emotions and nostalgia. *Earth* was associated with snow and ice; with midnight, endings and the season of winter. In human life, Earth heralds ageing and death. Other correspondences are wisdom, consolidation and rebirth.

Modern science seems to have abandoned the alchemical version of elemental principles in favour of new systems for organising the forces of the world into comprehensive tables and charts. The basic building blocks, however, do correspond to the older system. Earth has become carbon; Water, hydrogen; Air, oxygen; and Fire, nitrogen. The table of elements in modern chemistry proceeds from these basic four principles. Similarly, energy is seen as existing in different states — solid, liquid, gaseous and plasmic, with all forms of matter consisting of varieties and harmonies of these energies.

There is a coherence in all these ways of describing the building blocks which compose our realities. Each of the Elements (Air, Fire, Water and Earth) works symbolically and represents a different combination of physical, emotional and etheric correspondences. Working with the Elements enables us to balance the divergent aspects of our lives, and leads to greater internal harmony and integrity of purpose. Therefore, the first stones which we gather are the Elemental stones. Gathering these, working with, and casting them enables us to examine the patterns in our life. Making use of these symbols for divination is like painting in the background of a picture in broad strokes of the brush. They provide a starting place which our remote ancestors would have understood as representing the forces of nature, and which philosophers of various ages in human history would have comprehended as representing the esoteric elements.

The aim of *Dreamstones* is to integrate the elements of the self, to reconnect with the magic of the living earth. This connection is expressed in Rachel Bradley's *Dragonshadow*:

Nexus

The places of my past
call me
to my older selves —
with the Geomancer's sense of springs
hidden deep, and sacred sites,
I have not quite forgotten

Déjà vu
— walking the great stone circles
and ancient forests of Albion
— the bleached stony hills of Greece,
the scent of the dark bleak cypress
— the heights of defeated Macedon,
thyme crushed between fingers in
elusive pungency

Nexus —
time to time, time within time —
some Self, this not-quite-stranger
within me, bridges
the millennia
and all that's passed between is
only the shadow of Mortality

ELEMENTAL SYMBOLS

The following Elemental symbols are taken from alchemy (the origin of modern chemistry). Everything in the Universe consists of various quantities of these Elements — and every psychological state and energy pattern is related to one or more of the Elemental energies. You will notice that these symbols appear at the top of the Key Associations (one-word Keys for the stones) for the Stone Pentacle, and also appear on the Keys for the Three Rings (eighteen stones which proceed from the Stone Pentacle). When you see these symbols associated with a particular stone in the Three Rings, you will know that the stone in question is an amplification of this elemental energy, though it will, of course, contain other qualities which are particular to its own sphere of influence. In addition the symbol for Spirit is given; this symbol will appear on Keys for stones which contain vibrations of the energy of Spirit.

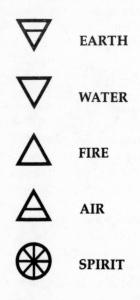

EARTH

WATER

FIRE

AIR

SPIRIT

Chapter 7
WORKING WITH ENERGY

There are two main ways of working with the energy of the Dreamstones: the first is in choosing the stones which we associate with the different elements and aspects of our lives; and the second is in deliberately 'charging' these stones with our own energy.

In the first instance, we utilise our senses (both physical and intuitive) to select the ones with an inherent energy which appeals to us in some way. Then we refine our selection to those stones which resonate with the internal concept we have of a particular idea. My stone for Earth, for example, was chosen after much deliberation. First I chose, by colour, size and aesthetic senses, a number of stones which looked like my concept of Earth; then I closed my eyes and touched each stone in turn, gradually sorting until there were only two to chose from; and the final selection was made by placing each stone on my forehead (the third eye), and then behind my ear, against the skull (almost like listening for the resonance of the stone against my own bones). This process gave me information from a combination of senses and narrowed the selection down to the particular stone which is my Earth Stone. Most of the other stones in my collection were chosen in a similar fashion, with a couple of exceptions in stones which were gifts from various people. A friend recently mentioned that, in her experience, some people do not have a proper sense of the energies of an object until they have touched it to their tongue, which is not something I had thought of before; however, it makes perfect sense to add this technique if it makes it easier to make a decision on the right stones.

The second way of working with the Dreamstones is to add to their intrinsic energy by formulating a relationship with each stone. We work with the energy of the stone, together with the energy of a particular aspect of our own personality, bonding the two together. These exercises are contained in Chapter 8, *The Stone Pentacle*, and in Chapter 11, *Dreamstone Circles*. Therefore, by working with a combination of stones, we also work with the corresponding aspects of our own inner nature, and are able to consciously explore the complex patterns in our lives. The self-knowledge which comes from this exploration is intended, in time, to result in a transformation of the Self into a more integrated and flexible being.

STORING THE STONES

One aspect of creating a relationship with your stones is in the practical actions necessary to store, cleanse, protect and care for them. Stones store and gather impressions from handling and should be kept in a special bag, pouch or box to protect them from random (unwanted) influences. Silk is a traditional insulating agent; however, chamois, leather or any natural fibre is also suitable. If you are particularly attracted to a synthetic fibre as an outer covering for your pouch, then line it with silk or cotton, so that the natural fibre rests against the stones. When you gather the first stones (Yes, No and Question — plus the stones of the Stone Pentacle) you should carry them with you at all times to attune yourself to their energy and create the special relationship necessary for inspired stonecasting. Therefore, a leather or cloth pouch worn around the neck or tied at the waist (worn on a long thong, hidden inside your clothing) is a good notion.

The simplest pouch is made from soft leather or suede and consists of a circle six inches in diameter with holes punched around the outside, approximately a quarter-inch from the rim. A leather thong is threaded through the holes, and the circle is drawn in to make a pouch. Another simple pouch is made from two pieces of material (leather, suede, cotton, etc.) which are sewn together, with a drawstring at the neck. Alternatively, a natural material such as wood, shell or bone, perhaps a ceramic container, a marble or onyx box, would be appropriate. In this you are limited only by your imagination, and restricted to selection of natural materials.

The stones you gather will be of different hardnesses, which can lead to some becoming worn away, chipped, or broken by others. This can be guarded against by having small pockets, sewn into the lining of the pouch, into which you can place the softer stones so that they do not rub against the harder ones. If the stones are a very smooth, regular shape, or are spherical or egg-shaped, this wearing down will be reduced as fewer surface areas will come into close contact.

I have a carved wooden container to store my stones at home, and when I travel I put them into a leather bag which is decorated with bone and shell. Both containers have been 'charged' by the power of concentration, and by applying protective symbols to them in a ritual.

CLEANSING

Cleansing of your stones includes both physical and psychic techniques. Physical cleansing involves washing the stones in salt water, then in pure spring or rain water, and polishing them with a soft, clean cloth. The salt and fresh water also acts to clean unwanted outside influences from the stone, so it can be the first thing you do with your stones when you bring them home — whether from the beach, a riverbed or a local lapidary shop. It is often difficult to get a clear impression of the intrinsic qualities of a stone until the influences of other people who have handled it have been cleared away; the process of physical cleansing will achieve this. A couple of drops of essential oil of jasmine (clarity) or rosemary (protection) added to the fresh water will take away from the stone any lingering traces of other people's energy.

It may be necessary to cleanse the stone of unwanted personal emotions as well. An example was related by a friend, where a person had a favourite crystal which was worn on a thong around the neck throughout their waking hours and removed while they slept. They would constantly touch the stone, especially in times of stress. Unfortunately they had experienced a situation where there was a lot of anger directed at them, and where they had reacted with anger of their own. This was inadvertently concentrated into the stone, which they were holding at the time. For days afterwards, they felt edgy, and eventually became quite depressed; the feelings only went away at night. The problem was diagnosed by someone else who noticed their connection with the crystal. A cleansing of the stone in salt water, deliberately willing away the negative influence which it had gathered, rebalanced the crystal and lifted the person's mood again, as they were no longer reacting to an old anger which had been concentrated in the stone. Most crystal lore will emphasise the ability of these stones to clear anger and transform negativity; however, they do have to be programmed to do so.

The positive power of anger well-expressed can be deliberately bound into an active stone to enhance personal assertiveness and self-determination. However, emotions which are not focused and directed positively can be picked up by your casting stones if you are holding them when you have such an experience. If the stone is within your body field, but protected by a special bag, this is much less likely to occur; the stones you carry with you will then pick up only the vibrations to which you have programmed them to be sensitive. It is a useful practice to periodically cleanse your stones, much as an artist will thoroughly clean his brushes from time to time, or a writer will clear the desk and file papers which have accumulated. This cleansing re-affirms your link with the stones (or crystals) and neutralises other energies with which they have come into contact. The following words can be said while concentrating on combining rock-salt and water for cleansing of your stones:

> *May this pure water be joined with the power of salt, that it may cleanse and bless these stones of the Living Earth.*

PROTECTION

Runes or symbols of protection or magic can be sewn or painted onto cloth bags, and painted or carved onto containers which hold your stones. If you 'charge' a special container for your stones, it will gather energy from them, creating a place of comfortable resonance. The container becomes more resonant over a period of time and sends its vibrations out into the room, weaving a subtle tapestry of energies in your immediate environment. All that is necessary in consecrating or 'charging' the container is a focusing of your will and concentration on the object, imagining it as a place of positive energies, of protection, containment and harmony.

CHARGING THE STONES

A 'charged' stone is essentially an amulet or talisman which represents, in a symbolic manner, the qualities with which you have energised it. As Paul Beyerl has said in his book, *The Master Book of Herbalism*:

> 'Humans, and they are not the only creatures on Earth who do so, are continually fascinated with brightly coloured stones which look different from the rest of the surroundings. They pick them up, put them safely in a pocket, and, even as time moves on, keep them as a source of enchantment and wonder. There are few of us who have not collected feathers, bits of string, or other curiosities on our journeys. These are the ingredients for the traditional amulet.'

Each stone should be cleansed and blessed as you would any object of power or tool of magic or healing. The Dreamstones are 'charged' in a process of concentrating certain information into them, such as the symbols or associations which represent the qualities of each particular stone. Herbs can be utilised to unlock a comprehension of the powers of a particular stone, and a tea made from an appropriate herb (see Key Associations in Chapter 13 for special herbs associated with each stone) can, when ingested while concentrating on a stone, help in bringing about insights on the inner nature of both the stone and its associated qualities. A tea is made by steeping an appropriate (and non-poisonous) herb in boiling water for five to ten minutes. Note that care should be taken to check the qualities of that herb in a reliable herb book, to ensure that its properties are not likely to upset your particular digestive system, or prove dangerous when combined with any other medication you may be taking.

Similarly, essential oils (available in some esoteric bookshops and herbalist dispensaries) can be burned as incense on charcoal blocks to both alter your consciousness to the desired vibration, and charge the stone with the desired qualities by passing the stone through the rising smoke. The combination of scent and concentration on the images and symbols connected with a stone affix Key Associations in your mind, which are easily recalled when interpreting the meaning of a stone in a casting. This is important — a diviner who has to look up a book for meanings quickly loses credibility!

When 'charging' a stone, you concentrate all your energies on what that stone represents to you. When it has been cleansed in salt water and polished on a cloth, you begin to work with it, using the exercises given for the Stone Pentacle or creating your own exercises inspired by your own dreaming, and store it in your special pouch or container before moving on to the next stone in the sequence.

There is a simple ritual at the end of each of the Stone Pentacle elements and at the end of the Three Rings, which you may choose to perform when integrating the energies of each new set of stones. These ritual actions concentrate your attention on the interconnections between the stones, and emphasise the balance of energies both in the stones and in the world around you.

Chapter 8
THE STONE PENTACLE

The Pentacle is a symbol which represents cosmic man, a figure in balance. We are familiar with Leonardo Da Vinci's drawing of a man superimposed on this figure, and with various talismans which incorporate it. The silver Pentacle is often used by modern esoteric traditions as a recognition sign, and embellishments or designs based around it are common. It is synonymous with the notion of magic and mystery. In the tarot, Pentacles are governed by the element of Earth, with various interpretations of balance, wealth, growth and protection.

The five stones which make up the Stone Pentacle are elements in your life which are equally important. If you neglect Spirit, you deny connection with the revitalising energy of the cosmos; neglect Fire, and your self worth and sexuality declines; neglect Water and your emotions will be out of balance; if you neglect Air, then you do not give credit to your intelligence and ability to make clear decisions; and if you do not pay attention to Earth, then it is difficult to support yourself financially, to maintain your health and to find enjoyment in sensuality.

The aim of the Stone Pentacle is to balance the major facets of your life, so that you are aware of the areas which need work and attention. Then, when these major areas are in balance in your own life, you are able to interpret the stones for friends. Self-knowledge, observation and the ability to accurately interpret the balance of forces in your own, and another's, life are the hallmarks of a good reader of the Oracle.

From these beginnings, proceed to the more in-depth interpretations which utilise the full Oracle of over twenty individual stones.

EARTH

Think of the ground beneath your feet, the weight of your body, the bones which form your skeletal structure, your nails, teeth and hair. The Element of Earth relates to that part of your spirit which is the Land Self.

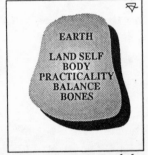

The Land Self has its part in the food chain, the web of life, the organic and symbiotic relationship with the land. It is where you derive your sense of place, home and sensuality — the enjoyment of the body and the senses. The Land Self remembers the home and experiences the lessons of survival. Here is wisdom, stability, personal integrity and the prosperity and fruitfulness of the harvest.

Because the land gives us sustenance, the Element of Earth is associated with plenty, abundance, fertility and wealth. Thus, an Earth Stone represents property, finances, business, balance and practicality. The Land Self governs that part of your life concerned with health, nutrition, working and physical activity.

48

Working with Earth

Choose a stone for Earth which makes you feel stable, balanced and comfortable. Purify the stone by burying it in the ground for a few days, followed by rubbing it with salt. Salt is associated with the Element of Earth because it improves the taste of food, preserves it and has been used as a measure of wealth.

Hold your Earth Stone in your hand while exercising, enjoying physical pursuits such as eating, and walking. Earth is also the element of repose, of rest and waiting, and thus governs sleep. Record your impressions in your journal and carry the stone with you during your daily activities. Make a conscious effort to notice the practical, Earth aspects of your everyday life.

Stones of Earth

Some stones which balance the powers of Earth are Haematite, Obsidian, Smokey Quartz, Jasper, Fossils and Petrified Wood.

My thoughts on Earth:

WATER

Be aware of your blood, saliva, urine, sexual fluids and tears, of your emotions and instinctive responses to the world around you. The Sea Self answers to the rhythm of the tide in your blood, which in turn responds to the call of the Moon. The Sea Self remembers the amniotic fluid of the womb and the primal sea of dreams. Here is the realm of feelings and mystical insights.

WATER

SEA SELF
FEELINGS
EMOTIONS
RELATING
FLUIDS

The Sea Self responds to myth, poetry and music. The element of Water is associated with dreams, visions and scrying. It is your sympathy and understanding of another's inner Self, the ability to listen and comprehend the underlying meaning of a situation. Hence, counsellors have a strong water aspect.

The tide in your blood links you to all other organic life which heeds the same call. The element of Water is your unconscious, primal Sea Self which is intuitional, empathic and nurturing. The Sea Self reflects the moods and changes of the ocean and is concerned with relationships, mirrors and images of reality. It is contemplative and concerned with matters of love, friendship and harmony.

Working with Water

Choose a stone for Water which appeals to your intuition and emotions. Bathe it in the waters of the sea and a river or mineral spring. Anoint it with the fluids of your body and cherish it with your feelings of care and harmony. Hold it in your hand while you play your favourite music; place it in a bowl of water and see how it changes with the reflections and distortions of the water covering it. Remember your dreams and record them in your journal. Be aware of your emotional responses; listen to your Sea Self and move instinctively through your life.

Stones of Water

Some stones which contain and reflect the images of water are Lapis Lazuli, Turquoise, Agate, Amethyst and Jade.

My Thoughts on Water:

FIRE

Think of your vital energy, the firing of nerves to send messages around the body, the passion and lust for life which gives you purpose and drive. The Fire Self is volatile, creative and dynamic and represents the realm of energy.

Here the contained tension manifests as a generative process where the twin arts of creative expression and disciplined will be found. The Fire Self awakens with the onset of puberty and shows itself in your sexuality, ambition and personal power. It is the will to achieve, and the energy which burns away the dross to find the kernel of individual strength within.

The element of Fire governs sexual attraction, healing and the spirit of adventure. Primal Fire sparks activity and change. It is that part of your spirit which is attracted to the colourful and challenging things in life. Fire is the element of the lifeforce and thus governs health, imagination and self-image. It is the heart of your individuality.

Working with Fire

Choose a stone for fire which stimulates your energy and imagination. Anoint it with an essential oil, such as patchouli, cinnamon or clove, and focus your will and personal energy on making a connection with the force that lives inside the stone and yourself. Introduce the stone to candle-light and hold it in your hand when you are watching a fire; keep it close to you during sexual activity; and record your impressions of fire in your journal. Be aware of your ambitions, personal power and dynamic energy, as well as the tensions in your life which generate change. Examine your will and creativity.

Stones of Fire

Some stones which generate the energy of fire are Carnelian, Garnet, Jasper, Bloodstone and red/orange/gold Agate.

My Thoughts on Fire:

AIR

Think of the breath of life, the flow of oxygen into your lungs and the clarity of intellect. The Element of Air relates to the Talking Self who is gifted with the power of words and ideas, the ability to express new concepts and communicate with others.

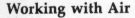

The Talking Self is concerned with your place in society, your educational standing and ability to articulate your personal needs. Air rules thaumaturgy (magic), ritual, travel, writing, musical composition and song. It represents the linear and organised thought processes, as well as inspiration, and is the predominant element in many scientists, researchers, mathematicians, media publicists and systems analysts.

The Talking Self is your conscious, Waking Self and some of its attributes are humour and quick wit. Air is the realm of law, politics, entertainment and changing social structures.

Working with Air

Choose a stone for Air which stimulates your intellect and clarifies your thoughts. Choose an incense such as sage, which clears the mind, or jasmine, which focuses the attention, and use it to concentrate on the powers of Air. Purify your stone by passing it through the incense smoke.

Hold the stone in your hand as you walk in the force of a windy day; breathe on it with the intention of 'charging' it with the power of your breath. Place it on your forehead for a few moments before sleep and know that it will bring clarity to your dreaming. Record your impressions in your journal and pay close attention to your changing ideas and decisions. Discover how the Element of Air works in your own psyche and learn new lessons from your work.

Stones of Air

Some stones which focus the Element of Air are Herkimer Diamonds, Rutilated Quartz, Chalcedony and Tiger's-Eye.

My Thoughts on Air:

SPIRIT

Perceive how your body, mind, emotions and energy work together as a whole. The unique character of their interaction is the realm of your Spirit. It is partly the sum of your experiences, coupled with the subjective relationship you have with the world around you. However, the Spirit Stone represents your deepest connection with the creative powers of the universe.

Your Spiritual Self is non-material, but manifests itself through your material body and thus partakes of both the world of man and the world of Faerie. It is connected with the unseen, hidden mysteries of the world and represents the resonance of your true, integrated Self.

Working with Spirit

Imagine yourself as a radiant being, absorbing the light of the cosmos, and become more aware, radiant and conscious of your actions, thoughts, feelings and sensations.

Choose a stone for Spirit which represents the synthesis of your true Self, that which you will become. Contemplate your centre and find a symbol in your imagination which represents that centre (a nautilus shell, a stone, a flower, a spider's web — whatever you find as your own symbol). Project that image through the stone to awaken the resonance of your spirit within the gem.

Using a crystal, focus light on the Spirit Stone — the refractions of the crystal will bathe your stone with the colours of the spectrum. The Spirit Stone represents the full spectrum, the integrated Self, radiant and beautiful.

Before you sleep, hold the Spirit Stone over each of your body's energy centres (genitals, belly, solar plexus, heart, throat, forehead and crown of head — i.e. the chakras), and then place it beneath your pillow while you sleep and dream. When you wake, record your dreams in your journal, for these are the voice of your Spirit speaking to your deep Self.

Stones of Spirit

Some stones which focus the brilliance of your Spirit are Opals, Herkimer Diamonds, Rainbow Crystals, Icelandic Spar, Silver-Sheen Obsidian and any other stone which you find resonates to your highest ideals. For this stone especially, the choice is a very personal one.

My Thoughts on Spirit:

ENERGISING THE STONE PENTACLE

Gather a bowl of rich earth and five candles (small slim votive candles are probably best — choose appropriate colours to be associated with the five elemental stones); find a time which is quiet and a place where you will not be distracted.

Breathing deeply and evenly, centre your energies and join the energy of the stones together by concentrating on their properties as you place them in sequence on the pattern. Name each stone in turn with words of your choice, stating the Key Associations and qualities you sense about that stone; light a votive candle beside each one, allowing it to burn while you meditate on the qualities of the stones and their relationships with each other stone in the pattern. These candles may then be extinguished and kept in a special place, ready to be burned again whenever you wish to add more energy to the stone which is resonant with a particular candle — write or inscribe the name of the stone onto the candle. The Mandala below shows the pattern in which you should place the Dreamstones:

Mandala — The Stone Pentacle

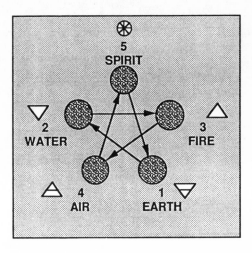

Key Associations

The Key words associated with each element are shown at the beginning of each section. The following chart shows the Four Elements plus Spirit, together with their Key Associations.

EARTH	WATER	FIRE	AIR	SPIRIT
LAND SELF	SEA SELF	FIRE SELF	TALKING SELF	HIGHER SELF
BODY	FEELINGS	WILL	INTELLECT	RADIANCE
PRACTICALITY	EMOTIONS	SEXUALITY	MIND	INTEGRATION
BALANCE	RELATING	CREATIVITY	CLARITY	SYNTHESIS
BONES	FLUIDS	ENERGY	BREATH	SOUL

Chapter 9
CASTING THE STONES

You have now gathered, charged and worked with your Elemental stones, and know how they represent aspects of the Self. By casting the five stones which make up the Stone Pentacle, you will be able to see how the elemental energies intertwine to form relationships in your own life.

There are a few important things to remember when casting the stones, of which being in the right frame of mind is probably the most important. Settling yourself, putting extraneous concerns to one side, being physically and emotionally centred — all these things are necessary in enabling you to hear clearly the voice of the Oracle. The following check-list should assist you:

1 *Are you hungry, thirsty or overtired?*
2 *Do you feel relaxed? Alert? Awake?*
3 *Do you really want an answer to your question?*
4 *Is this an appropriate time to cast the stones?*

THE SETTING

For your first casting find a quiet, secluded place, where you can sit comfortably on the ground. Close your eyes and take a few deep breaths, feeling energy fill your lungs. Place your hands on your belly, a couple of inches below your navel, and feel the warm glow radiating from that spot. Your energy centre, your place of balance, is approximately three fingers down from the navel and three inches inside the body.

Pay attention to how your energy gathers and moves to and from your centre. Place your tongue just behind your upper teeth and breathe slowly and evenly through your nose. Feel how this increases your feelings of strength and balance. Feel the energy flow through your body, unlocking areas of tension and discomfort, calming your emotions and thoughts.

ENERGISING THE STONES

Ask yourself which is your 'giving' hand (the hand with which you send out energy into the world), and which is your 'receiving' hand (the one you receive energies with). It may help to know that many occultists, esoteric healers and diviners work on the premise that the left side of the body is negative (receiving) and the right side is positive (giving). However, this is not a hard and fast rule; if the reverse demonstrably works best for you, then you should flow with that self-knowledge.

Place the stones in your 'receiving' hand, as you are going to send energy and a question to the stones. Concentrate attention on your centre and, taking three deep breaths, fill yourself with energy. Send that energy to your 'receiving' hand and into the stones. Imagine the stones becoming sensitised to the question you are about to frame, and ask *'What area of my spirit needs my attention today?'*.

Pour the stones into your 'giving' hand, imagining the answer being formulated. Take another three deep breaths and send the energy from your centre to your 'giving' hand, filling the stones with power.

Slowly, and with concentration, pour the stones from hand to hand, imagining the connection between 'receiving' the question and 'giving' the answer. Imagine a line of blue fire making a circuit from your centre to your hands, and then to the stones.

THE CAST

When you feel that the stones are 'humming' or 'vibrating' with energy, and you are ready and centred within yourself, cast the stones onto the ground or onto a specially prepared casting cloth, using a serpentine sweep of your cupped hands.

You may then choose to close your eyes and move the stones with your hands until you feel comfortable with their placement. Open your eyes and ready yourself to begin interpreting the patterns and relationships formed by the stones.

INTERPRETATION

Take another three deep breaths and quietly gaze at the stones, noting their different positions. In the next chapter I discuss the process of recording and interpreting the fall of stones, so I will not go into detail here. A quiet and reflective frame of mind, alert and aware but relaxed, not straining for information, is the state of consciousness you are aiming for at this stage of stonecasting. With practice, you will be able to enter this state whenever you trigger it by casting your stones.

CLOSING THE PATTERN

Casting the stones is a small ritual which should be formally closed, and its energy grounded, otherwise you could find yourself helplessly interpreting random patterns around you, which affects your judgement of reality. Too much sensory information can be damaging to personal balance. This can be a fine thing to do if you are wanting to see deeply into nature, but too distracting if you have a need to accomplish anything that day.

A Way of Closing

Gather the Dreamstones in your cupped hands. Close your hands together and raise them to your mouth. Take a deep breath and, as you inhale, feel the breath energising your body, gathering power in your centre. As you exhale, imagine a stream of energy rising from your centre to your throat, then to a place behind your eyes. Feel the realisation of your reading concentrate there. Blow your breath out through your mouth, onto the stones, and imagine them being cleansed and recharged. Do this three times.

Store your stones carefully in their own pouch or bag and take the realisation of your question into your life for the day. Work with the area of your spirit which wished conversation with you and learn to recognise how your own Essential Being communicates with you through divinatory techniques.

When you have put your stones away carefully, wash your hands in cold water, clap them together a couple of times or rub them briskly. Get up and move around. Have a good stretch and do something practical and grounding such as making a cup of tea or a meal.

When you have worked with the Stone Pentacle and feel confident in your interpretations of patterns in your own life, you can (a) begin to work with the next set of stones and design your own exercises, and (b) start to consult the Oracle for your friends. The Dreamstone Pentacle, once balanced, provides the basis for further readings.

Chapter 10
INTERPRETING THE ORACLE

In consulting the Oracle, you open your awareness to the patterns in the universe, finding your interpretation in your personal experiences and the knowledge gained by working with combinations of stones.

There are two basic environments for interpretation: you will either be casting and interpreting for yourself, or for another querent. These situations require quite a different approach to interpretation. In divining for yourself, the primary goal is self-analysis, using the patterns of the stones to discover which elements of your life are out of balance, so that you might take action to re-harmonise those things. In divining for someone else you have a responsibility to act as the voice of the Oracle, presenting a different perspective on their life so that they might make decisions and/or changes.

INTERPRETATION FOR THE SELF — A STONE JOURNAL

The following sample readings take the recording of a personal stonecasting step by step. The sequence for recording your own stonecasting allows you to make a cursory, first glance interpretation and progress from there into complex interpretations with more than the three stones of *Beginning Divination*, or the five stones of the *Stone Pentacle*.

INTERPRETATION FOR ANOTHER PERSON

The Spirit Stone can represent another person. Take the Spirit Stone in your 'receiving' hand and concentrate on your feelings, ideas and images of that person. If they are present, they can hold the stones in their cupped hands and breathe on them. This temporarily places their energy on the stones, which you can remove later by breathing your own energy into them.

However, you may not feel comfortable with someone else touching your stones. If this is the case, listen to your inner voice to decide how to proceed. Usually, this means you should energise the stones for the reading yourself, as above.

Follow the usual practice for casting the stones and ask the question 'What is happening in X's life right now?' or 'What area of X's spirit should they pay attention to today?'. Then proceed, as you would for yourself, with an interpretation of the cast. A word of caution — keep an open mind about the meaning of the cast in relation to someone else, as their priorities in life will not necessarily be the same as yours. As a diviner you are in the responsible position of confidant/e, counsellor or confessor. Your responsibility is to listen, to provide an accurate and knowledgeable interpretation of the Oracle, and to assist the querent to perceive the priorities and decisions which surround them in a clear manner. You are *not* there to make decisions for them or to replace their own sense of correct behaviour, or to pass judgement on them. Your responsibility as a Diviner is to make people aware of the overall patterns in their lives; judgement of those patterns is up to them, personally.

GUIDELINES FOR INTERPRETATION

To summarise, some basic guidelines in interpreting the Oracle for another person are:

1 Be non-judgmental.
2 Listen carefully (with all your senses).
3 Interpret tactfully and responsibly.
4 Be positive and, if necessary, entertaining.
5 Highlight positive aspects of the stonecasting and provide your insight in dealing with difficult aspects of a casting.
6 Maintain confidentiality.

A STONE JOURNAL

The following pages give step-by-step guidelines for keeping a journal to record the casting of the Dreamstones.

STONE JOURNAL

(1)
DAY OF WEEK   DATE   SEASON

MOON PHASE   DAY OF CYCLE

(2) TODAY'S STONE CASTING

(3)
1. Stone closest to Spirit Stone:_____

2. The issue is: _____

3. Stone furthest from Spirit Stone:_____

4. Is it an avoidance issue? ☐ Unimportant? ☐

5. Comment:_____

(4A) INTERPRETATIONS

(4B) GETTING YOUR ROCKS OFF

6. Image: _____

7. The image suggests: _____

8. Stone Relationships:

(5) COURSE OF ACTION

(6) Unfinished Business ...

PAGE #

63

① Date and Time of Reading

Keeping a record of the day of week, date, season and moon phase enables you to look back over your records and identify patterns: for example, do particular balances within your psyche change according to the phase of the moon, the day of the week or the season of the year? For women, keeping a record of the day of menstrual cycle will give added insight into your psychic sensitivity. Men can gauge their sensitivity by the moon's phases (though if they are living with a sensitive woman, her cycle may also affect them).

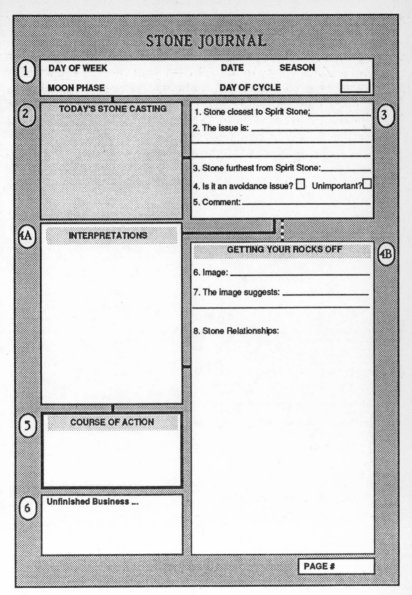

② Today's Stonecasting

Draw a diagram of the pattern of stones which you have cast. This will allow you to go back and check aspects of stones at the end of the day in order to validate your interpretation.

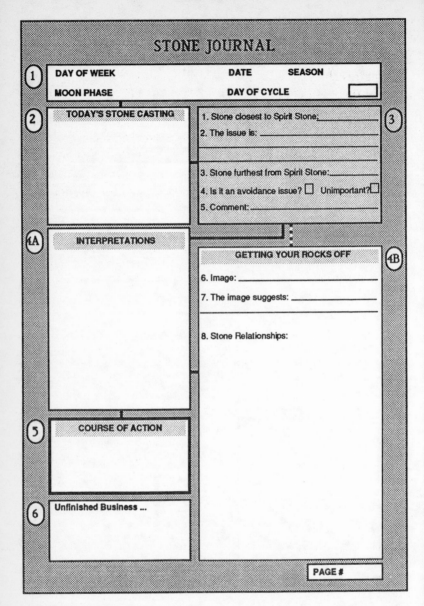

STONE JOURNAL

① DAY OF WEEK | DATE | SEASON
MOON PHASE | DAY OF CYCLE

② TODAY'S STONE CASTING

③ 1. Stone closest to Spirit Stone:_____
2. The issue is: _____

3. Stone furthest from Spirit Stone:_____
4. Is it an avoidance issue? ☐ Unimportant?☐
5. Comment:_____

④A INTERPRETATIONS

④B GETTING YOUR ROCKS OFF
6. Image: _____
7. The image suggests: _____

8. Stone Relationships:

⑤ COURSE OF ACTION

⑥ Unfinished Business ...

PAGE #

③ **Information**

This section (*1-5 below*) is the minimum information you need in order to interpret the Dreamstones.

66

1 Stone Closest to Spirit Stone

This is the obvious answer to your question — the stone has fallen into proximity with your Spirit Stone. Fill in the blank space on the page.

2 The Issue

Ask yourself what that stone means to you; this indicates what area of your spirit needs attention for the day. This is the issue.

    Are there two stones equally close to the Spirit Stone? Then both those areas need looking at; individually and together. The stones closest to Spirit are the most important focal points in your life at this time.

3 Stone Furthest from Spirit Stone

Fill in the blank space on the page to denote the stone which is furthest from Spirit.

4 Avoidance or Unimportant?

Look at the meaning for this stone. Does it relate to an issue which you are avoiding? Or is it simply not important to you at the moment? It may be a part of the Self or a part of your surroundings which you feel quite comfortable with, and which is therefore not a current issue.

5 Comment

This space is for commenting further on (4) above, with space for a few words to expand on the stone furthest away as being either something you are avoiding, or something unimportant.

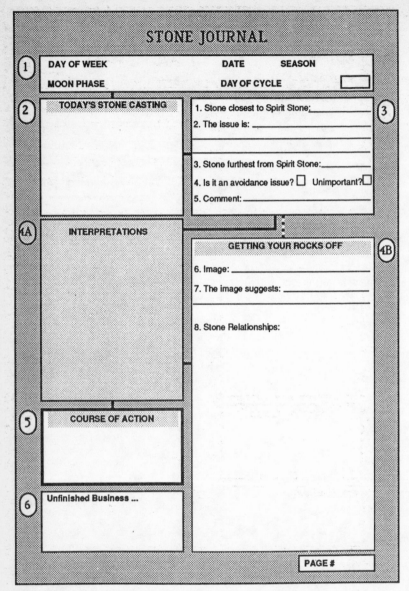

④A Interpretations

Here you write your interpretation (story-line) of the casting. What do the issue and surrounding elements signify to you?

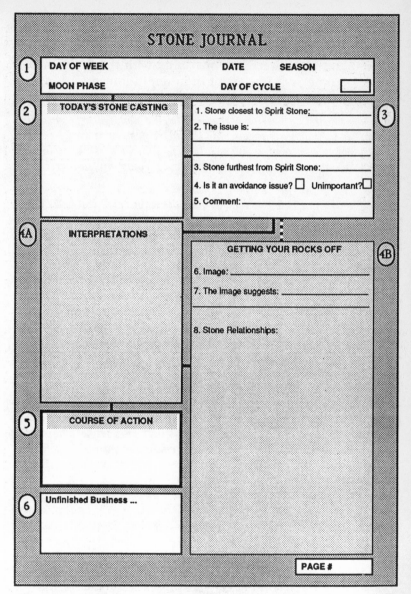

STONE JOURNAL

① DAY OF WEEK   DATE   SEASON

MOON PHASE   DAY OF CYCLE

② TODAY'S STONE CASTING

③ 1. Stone closest to Spirit Stone:_____

2. The issue is: _____

_____

3. Stone furthest from Spirit Stone:_____

4. Is it an avoidance issue? ☐   Unimportant?☐

5. Comment: _____

④A INTERPRETATIONS

④B GETTING YOUR ROCKS OFF

6. Image: _____

7. The image suggests: _____

_____

8. Stone Relationships:

⑤ COURSE OF ACTION

⑥ Unfinished Business ...

PAGE #

④A **Interpretation and Getting Your Rocks Off**   ④B

The heading indicates a certain irreverence as the images you
see in stonecasting are often amusing or unlikely. This section

(*6 to 8 below*) concentrates on symbolic images you see in the casting (birds, fish, trees, etc.) and what those suggest to you. In addition, extra space is given for listing relationships of stones other than those directly in proximity with the Spirit Stone. These become very important in in-depth interpretation.

6 *Image*
What is your first impression of the cast? Do the stones make a particular pattern? Is the fall of stones curved? Circular? A straight line? Does the pattern look like, or remind you of, a bird, an animal, a fish or an insect? Write this impression in your journal, before going any further.

7 *The Image Suggests . . .*
What does the image tell you about your life right now? If it looks like a bird, for example, does that mean you are free from pressures; that you desire freedom; that you are planning on travel? Expand on the image to give more detail on the pattern and what it means to you at the present.

Non-material shapes represent abstract concepts. Straight lines denote tensions (which can be positive or negative), curves represent flowing energy and ease with events; circular patterns indicate harmonious aspects of your life; and widely scattered stones indicate diversity and, perhaps, a lack of cohesion. Squares usually denote decisions to be made and triangular shapes usually mean completion of projects. I have found that spirals indicate energy, and their direction (inward or outward) can tell you if energy is increasing or decreasing — being expended in the world, or quietly working within the Self.

Where the cast looks like a bird or animal, the qualities of that creature are present in your life at the time of the casting; for example, a horse can indicate freedom, or the desire for it, travel, changeability and the ability to ride the winds of change. Keep a record of these patterns in your journal to see how your life patterns alter over time.

If there is no particular pattern discernible, this is also important. It can mean that you are at a crossroads where no pattern is clear until you have made a decision on which way you will travel. It can also indicate indecision and confusion or a pause between events, where no action is yet possible. No action is indicated by the pattern, so you must rely on the position of the stones and their relationships with each other to indicate what events are at work at that time.

8 *Stone Relationships*
Relationships of two stones indicate either dichotomy or related issues; three stones means constructive creativity; four, consolidation and co-

operative effort, though it can also show obstinacy; five stones together are a challenge, something new, or travel; and six stones indicate cautious planning, precision and sometimes indicate a lack of spontaneity.

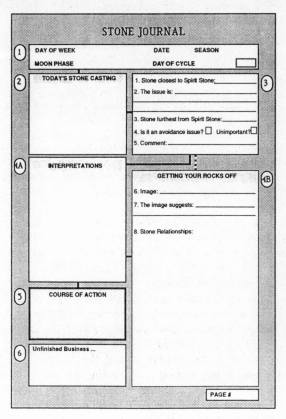

⑤ Course of Action

Following the interpretation, you will have certain courses of action open to you, ranging from ignoring the advice of the Oracle to taking action to resolve the issue indicated or balance a particular aspect of your personality.

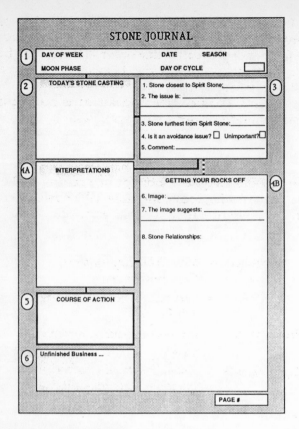

⑥ **Unfinished Business**

This space is intended for those things you meant to take action with but have not yet resolved; also any unresolved issues or events from the previous day.

PATTERNS IN STONE

When you cast the Dreamstones, patterns form which remind you of other patterns in the material and non-material world. Material patterns are those which look like leaves, trees, rivers, animals, birds, fish or insects; non-material patterns are shapes such as lines, curves and groups of stones, which may have no overriding familiarity to them. Material patterns borrow images from the natural objects, flora or fauna they seem to represent. In this way, a river pattern must have a source and an ending; the stones are read in that order. A tree is read from the roots (underlying cause) to the branches and leaves (the manifestation in the world).

In Interpreting the Stone Pentacle, some basic configurations and possible interpretations are as follows:

Pairs

Pairs are the first thing you look for in a casting of the Stone Pentacle. In particular, locate the stone which falls in conjunction with the Spirit Stone as this gives the focus of the casting.

Spirit/Air = *Ideas, Thinking Patterns,*
Communication.

Spirit/Fire = *Sexuality, Activity, Creativity,*
Self-Image.

Spirit/Water = *Emotions, Feelings, Relating,*
Dreams.

Spirit/Earth = *Home, Practicality, Money,*
Immediate Environment.

Trines

In the following Trines, the stone recorded immediately after the Spirit Stone is that closest to Spirit and is therefore the Issue of a stonecasting. The third stone in the trine gives valuable additional information on that Issue.

Spirit/Air/Fire = *Ideas/Creativity — new and*
innovative ideas which will
enhance your Self-Image.

Spirit/Fire/Air = *Creativity/Ideas — creativity*
and energy (Fire) is being
directed (Air); creative
inspiration and new ways of
expressing it; procrastination.

Spirit/Air/Water = *Ideas/Feelings — clarity of thought combined with emotional insight; being clear about the nature of your relationships.*

Spirit/Water/Air = *Relationships need to be thought out so that a clear direction can be found; self-questioning.*

Spirit/Air/Earth = *Ideas/Practicality — clear (Air) financial (Earth) direction; being careful about money, homelife, resources or health; caution in decision-making.*

Spirit/Earth/Air = *Practicality/Air — home reorganisation, spring cleaning, redecorating, organising paper-work; attending to details; organising legal matters.*

Spirit/Fire/Water = *Sexuality/Feelings — sexuality in relationships; creative dreams; arguments;*

Spirit/Water/Fire = *Feelings/Sexuality — romance, love and adventure; dreams providing inspiration for creativity.*

Spirit/Fire/Earth = *Creativity/Practicality — a creative project; a child's being conceived; creative actions with a lasting (Earth) result.*

Spirit/Earth/Fire = *Practicality/Energy — being practical about sexuality, creativity and available energy resources; attention to health and nervous tension.*

Spirit/Water/Earth = *Feelings/Stability — feelings are stable, and so too are friendships; a relationship which is getting deeper; a feeling of calm con-fidence and inner balance.*

Spirit/Earth/Water = *Stability/Feelings — home and feelings; a family relationship; buying a house; a commitment to a particular person; possibly getting bogged down and humourless in relating to others.*

The following sample castings give an indication of the flow of information from casting the stones to recording and interpreting the patterns. The Pairs and Trines above make patterns in the casting which can be aspected in different ways, depending on the placement of the other stones; the overall pattern gives an insight into the balance of forces on that particular day, allowing you to change elements which may be causing disharmonies.

Today's Stonecasting

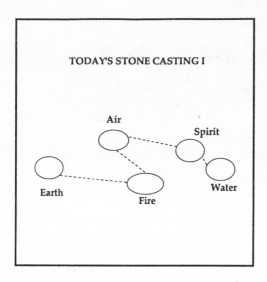

TODAY'S STONE CASTING I

Air

Spirit

Earth

Fire

Water

Information

1 *Stone Closest to Spirit Stone*
Water

2 *The Issue Is:*
Emotions, Feelings, Relating, Dreams.

3 *Stone Furthest from Spirit Stone*
Earth

4 *Is this an avoidance issue? Unimportant?*

5 *Comment:*
We will return to this in the interpretation.

Getting Your Rocks Off

6 *Image:*
Horizontal Pattern — person lying on their side

7 *The Image Suggests:*
A time of rest, or the need to do so, in order to pay attention to your emotions (the issue of the stonecasting).

Interpretations

Emotions and intuitions are the areas of your Spirit you most need to pay attention to. The pattern of the person lying on their side suggests that this is a reflective, rather than active, time for looking at how you relate to those people around you. It is also a time for examining your relationship with the Self through dreams.

The Fire Stone is the next closest stone, indicating a need to pay attention to energy levels and, relating it to the Water Stone, to examine sexuality and energy within relationships. The Air Stone is the next stone to look at, forming a close pattern (a downward pointing triangle, reminiscent of the symbol for Water, emphasising the power of emotion) with the Spirit and Fire Stones. I would interpret this pattern to mean that a specific relationship is being reconsidered (the Air qualities of clear thinking and decision-making) to see if a creative resolution (Fire) of blocked sexuality/energy can be found. Alternatively, it could mean a need to spend time alone

76

in order to recharge your own creativity and divert attention to your own emotional needs.

The Earth Stone is furthest away from the Spirit. This indicates that issues to do with finances, practical arrangements, everyday activities and work are distant. It can indicate that the emotional issues, which are of primary importance at the time of the stonecasting, are unbalancing you and placing strain on your stability.

Course of Action

It is important to maintain personal integrity and balance whilst applying your energy to self-healing. A reconsideration of your needs within relationships will lead to more energy being released. This, in turn, will enhance your creativity and enable you to communicate effectively with others. A time of rest will mean you can return to the world renewed.

Today's Stonecasting II

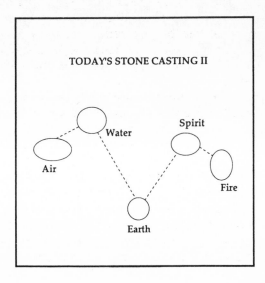

TODAY'S STONE CASTING II

Water

Spirit

Air

Fire

Earth

Information

1 Stone Closest to Spirit Stone
Fire

2 The Issue Is:
Sexuality, Activity, Creativity, Self-Image.

3 Stone Furthest from Spirit Stone
Air

4 Is this an avoidance issue? Unimportant?

5 Comment:
Could be a lack of concentration.

Getting Your Rocks Off

6 Image
Random pattern — a little like a bird in flight.

7 The Image Suggests:
Restlessness and dissatisfaction with surroundings. A need to move away from something, or towards a new adventure.

Interpretations

The Trine of Spirit/Fire/Earth usually suggests a creative project being conceived; however, the image of the bird in flight seems to indicate a lack of concentration (Air being the furthest stone from Spirit would tend to confirm this) or focus. There are a lot of ideas, and a tremendous amount of energy, but this needs to be concentrated into the one area before anything practical will result. Your surroundings will tend to be chaotic (Fire in relationship to Earth) and there is a tendency to avoid responsibility for emotional situations (Air + Water) due to impatience. Your temper will be a little uncertain for a while, until you feel more settled. This pattern (Spirit/Fire/Earth), if further emphasised by an active image (the bird), can also suggest sexual frustration, which may be affecting your self-image.

The sensuality of Earth, coupled with the sexuality of Fire and the impatience of needing a new creative outlet, can lead to seeking a new relationship, or more than one, to satisfy the craving for stimulation.

The distant Air and Water Stones suggest that rational

decisions about relationships are not something to concern yourself with today. Try not to have any serious 'heart-to-heart' discussions as you are likely to be contentious and stubborn, and disinclined to see another person's viewpoint. A day for activity, adventure and strenuous physical effort.

Course of Action

In order to feel more settled, allow yourself a holiday from responsibility for a day or so — you are not going to achieve much until you can concentrate, so you will feel more satisfied with life if you have an adventure. Creative projects around the house are a possibility, but only if they are quick changes to surroundings, as you will not have the patience to begin long and involved undertakings. A good time to travel, but take care not to become impatient with people. Seek the company of people you find exciting and challenging and try to temper your sense of adventure with a little common sense.

Part III
EXPLORING THE ORACLE

Chapter 11
DREAMSTONE CIRCLES

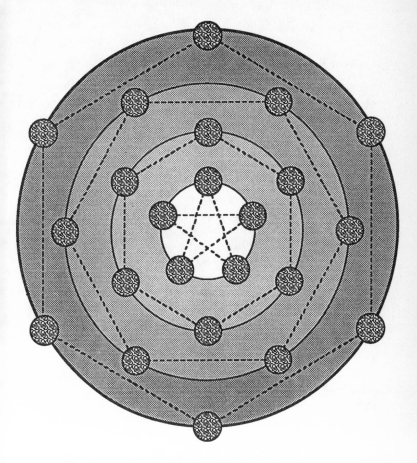

The next eighteen stones are arranged in Three Rings of stones, marking the increasing depth of your magical transformation. We explore each Ring in turn, and add each set to the Dreamstones in a measured fashion. If you started casting all the stones at once, right from the beginning, you would not be able to concentrate on the individual relationships between stones, or on those aspects of your own psyche which resonate with the same energies. Therefore, we start with the Yes, No and Question stones and proceed to the Stone Pentacle, adding the First Ring, then the Second and Third, until the set is complete. Treat each ring as a complete pattern and do not add it to your casting set until you have worked with the energies of all six stones in the Ring.

THE FIRST RING

The First Ring consists of stones representing the elements of life closest to the image of the Self. We explore the conscious (the Sun) and subconscious (the Moon) mind, the ability to communicate (Mercury) and relate to others (Venus), to identify with the natural environment and feel at home in our own body (Gaea), to express sexuality and power (Mars), to enjoy both harmonious existence and striving for achievement.

The First Ring is concerned with the everyday Self, the overall personality and surroundings the individual chooses for himself. It is the blueprint from which the deeper understandings proceed, and these areas are those which we find easiest to change and come to terms with in our life. If we feel good about ourselves, can identify our innermost needs, have an ability to communicate our ideas, have an appreciation for comfort and art, have a connection with the environment, and possess the energy to carry out our plans, then study of the patterns in life is possible. If any of these areas is out of balance, that area becomes a priority, and all other considerations are pushed to one side while we deal with the immediate personal needs. It is important to understand these areas, in association with the Stone Pentacle, so that we can compensate for stresses in our own lives when consulting the Oracle.

Stones of the FIRST RING are the *Sun, Moon, Mercury, Venus, Gaea* **and** *Mars*

THE SECOND RING

The Second Ring represents the powers of expansion (Jupiter) and contraction (Saturn), the dynamics of social systems and laws which govern group interaction. It is concerned with tensions which demand resolution, with the veils of illusion (Neptune) and inspiration (Uranus), and the transformation (Pluto) of the Phoenix, rising from the Fire of the Spirit. In this Ring, we approach the strands of Karma that weave our own actions into the universal tapestry, creating patterns for personal balance.

In the Second Ring, we deepen our connection with the energies which interpenetrate our psyche, the energies which are expressed in the world through our actions, our thoughts and relationship with others. Our place in society is explored, as are the disciplines and restrictions which act as a measure for personal morality. We travel in our journey beyond the personal into the world of transpersonal energies, which require others with whom to interact. We make the first steps towards dialogue with the Higher Self, and begin to work with the ability to claim power for self-transformation and personal balance.

Stones of the SECOND RING are *Jupiter, Saturn, Uranus, Neptune, Pluto* **and** *Karma.*

THE THIRD RING

The Third Ring consists of stones concerned with energic work — both our own energic actions as they manifest in the world, and the outer and random forces which exert their influences on our lives. The tides of our vitality and personal energy (Life) entwine with the power of emotional connection (Love), creating patterns to transcend individual consciousness. The force of energy (Magic), both disciplined and wild, is a gateway which we create to approach deity, and the polarised forces of Goddess and God work deep within the individual to effect growth and change. The last stone in this ring is one which is Random: it may represent luck, free energy, limitless possibilities or uncertain opportunities.

We travel deeper into the Self, and beyond the Self into the macrocosm, holding the inner and outer worlds in balance. The Third Ring is concerned with our deepest connections with the life-force, the seasonal cycles, the cosmic patterns which have been interpreted over the millennia as the outer manifestation of deity, fate and fortune. The Oracle speaks most clearly when we have worked with and understood the lessons of the Third Ring.

Stones of the THIRD RING are *Life,* *Love,* *Magic,* *Goddess, God* **and** *Random.*

DREAMSTONE MANDALAS

At the end of each section in the Three Rings, there is a Mandala created from a geometric placement of the stones on concentric rings of influence. The image in the centre is the Stone Pentacle, representing the most basic human needs; radiating outward from that are the Three Rings, representing the complexities which proceed from this central integration of energies — as you travel further outwards on the Mandala, you become more aware of deeper and more intricate influences which create your personal reality.

The First Ring

THE SUN

Ask yourself who you are and how you define your individuality. The Sun represents the Conscious Self, your vitality, strength and spiritual direction. In mythology, the Sun is associated with powerful Deities who are celebrated in all cultures, whether nomadic, hunter-gatherer, agricultural or technological. The division of day and night is often represented by a dichotomy of good and evil, with the light of day as the realm of the Bright Sun God.

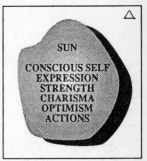

The Sun is associated with harvest celebrations and festivities, dance, music, the play of children, and celebration of life. The Sun is the Divine Child, reborn endlessly at midwinter solstice, and this child is part of yourself as child of the Deity. The Conscious Self is magnetic, attractive and generous in nature. It represents your self-expression and outward character. It is aware, alive, full of light and open to possibilities for drama, excitement and creative being.

The Conscious Self is active, intelligent and aware of who you want to be, of the impression you wish to make on others with whom you come into contact. The position of this stone in a reading shows how you express yourself and how you relate to the world around you.

The Key Words for the Sun are EXPRESSION and STRENGTH.

Stones of the Sun

Stones which amplify the energy of the sun are Citrine, Crysolite, Cat's-eye, Yellow Topaz, Rutilated Quartz and Amber.

My Thoughts on the Sun:

THE MOON

Ask yourself where you come from and how you relate to your ancestry, your personal background and memories. The Moon represents the subconscious Self, your feelings, impressions, relationship with inner mysteries and intuitive knowledge. The Moon Self is our hidden nature, secret and silent, who whispers from our dreams and is our inner guide.

In mythology, the Deities of the moon are dangerous and mysterious. They rule the night, mythic animals, dreams, lovers and the powers of divination. They change aspect with the changing faces of the moon, and influence the tides of the sea and of human love.

The Dreaming Self is identified with the myths of the moon maiden, mother and crone, who wax and wane with the lunar tides. It is also identified with Her lover, night hunter and primal shadow, those aspects of the night of the soul which is the reflection of our waking Selves. The Moon gives us the ability to find those people who feel akin to our own spirits, and to recognise them for their true Selves.

The position of this stone in a reading shows what your motivation is, how you feel about events and people around you and how clearly you are listening to your intuition.

The Key Words for the Moon are VISIONS and SECRETS.

Stones of the Moon

Stones which focus the intuitive powers of the moon are Moonstone, Pearl, Milky Agate, Amethyst and Aquamarine.

My Thoughts on the Moon:

MERCURY

Think of your ability to make decisions, to delineate a problem, define the parameters of a situation, to communicate clearly and effectively. These areas are ruled by Mercury, your Thinking Self.

Because this is a swift moving energy, and Mercury is a swift moving planet, this stone will also be associated with messages (both sacred and mundane), news and humour. The Thinking Self is rational and quick-witted, and, like a blade, words may also cut through to the heart of a situation. Surgeons, magicians, wizards and wanderers fall under the province of this energy, and so, too, do satirists, writers and salesmen.

The quicksilver twist of words, of piper, music and dance is expressed with your mercurial, changeable nature. The offspring of thought is the Child Self — who is always young, and ever ready to consider a new idea, game or strategy. Here is the innocent, the herald, the messenger of the Gods, who conveys the words of the Deity to humankind. We are made to understand by such myths the role of the messenger, who conveys but does not originate the message. In like manner, the rituals of religion and magic are theatre of the mind — a vehicle for travel, a communication, a guide to the mysteries, but not their substance. However, the initiate must have the ability to balance, to dance along the blade of life, in order to communicate with their Deity. We all have this ability, and with it the ability to research, to discriminate, to travel our own true path.

The position of this stone will tell you if you are making good decisions, and if you are able to articulate your ideas to others.

The Key Words for Mercury are MIND and COMMUNICATION.

Stones of Mercury

Mercurial stones are Ribbon Agate, Peridot, Tourmaline and Zircon. Another possibility (and a favourite of my own) is Gold Tiger's-Eye or stones with harlequin colours.

My Thoughts on Mercury:

VENUS

Ask yourself what kind of relation- ships you feel most comfortable with. Who are your friends? What do you desire i a lover? What makes you feel most sensual, pampered, loved? The Venus stone rules relationships of all kinds and your ability to co- operate with others within a social framework.

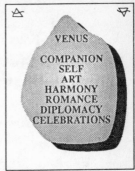

It is the part of your nature which is hospitable, creative in the home, appreciative of art, harmony and beauty. The Companion Self finds reward in association with others, in expressing harmony through art, celebration and friendship. The Companion Self is seductive, persuasive, understanding and empathic. A creative action of your choice should be incorporated into consecration of this stone — paint, draw, design, compose, cook, decorate, make clothes or wine, create a harmonious arrangement of your personal possessions. Keep the stone with you to absorb this energy of art and personal harmony.

Venus in Roman mythology (Aphrodite in Greek) is a Goddess of love. She is the courtesan who makes an art of love and the diplomat who makes an art of harmony. All acts of pleasure are her rituals, and she is the gateway to initiation through celebration of the body. However, her art cannot be reduced to simple gratification. This planetary energy is linked to positive and harmonious expression of the life principle, a channel for consummation of sacred love through internal balance and love of beauty. Venus is concerned with seduction and sensuality, with companionship, friendship and creativity. Venus balances the force of sexual energy to achieve creative and harmonious expression.

The position of this stone in a reading will show how well you understand others, and how you respond to pleasure in your life.

The Key Words for Venus are ART and HARMONY.

Stones of Venus

Stones which harmonise the energy of Venus are Malachite, Jade, Opal and Emerald. However, any particular stone which appeals to your aesthetic appreciation will be suitable.

My Thoughts on Venus:

GAEA

Gaea is the stone of the Earth Mother, of Nature in Her abundance. It signifies our connection with natural cycles, with home, health and environment. It is the stone which represents your place within the ecosystem and your sensitivity to planetary energies.

As you become more aware of your own personal needs and the activities which feel most comfortable for you, then the energy of the Earth will begin to flow through you to revitalise your body. Your ability to make a deep connection with special places and sacred sites is ruled by this stone. The Gaea stone is concerned with primal connections, instinctual behaviour and the animal consciousness which allows us all to feel the web of life, and our place within it. It is our Animal Self. We are able to exchange energies with the Earth: through trees and other plants as we breathe out carbon dioxide, receiving back oxygen; through our bodies; through magnetic currents; and by working with Her bones, the Dreamstones. The Gaea stone is the easiest stone to energise as it already contains the energy of the planet, gathered while it slumbered in the ground. To make a connection with Gaea, you join your Animal Self with the energy of the deep Earth. We do this by extending our everyday awareness to contact the energy of Gaea.

Working with Gaea

Take your Gaea stone outdoors while you walk barefoot on the grass and the soil. Stamp on the ground firmly, first one foot and then the other. Feel the vibration return to you from the Earth into your body, and then into the stone which you hold in your left hand. Walk amongst some leafy plants and feel them brush against you as you breathe deeply and inhale their cool green fragrance. Break a single leaf and rub it between the fingers of your right hand; then rub the juice of the plant on your Gaea stone. Sit beneath a tree and lean your back against it, feeling the rough texture against you. After a few moments, place your head back against the tree and close your eyes. Think about your relationship with the environment around you, and with the larger web of life, and feel the energy of that connection enter into the stone.

In Greek mythology, Gaea is a Goddess — however, she does not have the personality and human habits associated with most of their deities. The first representation of Her is of a female figure embedded in the ground, emerging only from breasts upwards. In most cases, however, she is symbolised by a local mountain, by the field of grain or tilled Earth, and by the mysterious powers of nature. She is the beautiful Earth, bountiful and generous, and also the terrible power of natural forces and disaster. The Gaea stone also has these two sides: in a stonecasting it can indicate great harmony and good fortune, or, conversely, alienation from the natural world, depending on how it is aspected.

In myth, it was the Serpent of Gaea which was subsumed by Apollo at Delphi. The Oracle then became interpreted by his priestesses. We should remember, however, that the site was sacred to Gaea first, and it was through contact with the venom of the serpents that the priestesses consulted the Oracle. The name of the Deity changed, but the power of nature, through connection with the Animal Self, remained.

The Gaea stone in a stonecasting indicates your state of emotional and physical balance, and connection with natural rhythms.

The Key Words for Gaea are NATURE and HOME.

Stones of Gaea

Any stone which you feel symbolises the energy of Gaea will be suitable. I have found Fossils, Blue/Gold Agate, Obsidian and Opal Matrix to be particularly attractive for this purpose, however you will no doubt find your own representation for Gaea based on a personal connection with Her energy.

My thoughts on Gaea:

MARS

Mars is the stone for energy, for raw, unbridled force, passion, sexuality and creativity. Feel your vital energies and health, the power of your muscles and surge of adrenalin which makes life exciting. Mars is the planet of struggle and conflict, and it is through the tension of this energy that we define our own personality in relation to others. Its martial strength may be

explored in a number of ways — through conflict and war, protection of loved ones, through striving to master your own creativity, in adventures and impulsive action, creation or destruction. It is impatient and immediate in its actions.

The Warrior Self will not fight unnecessary battles, and the power of this self lies in an ability to determine what is worth fighting for, and what is best left to peaceful resolution at another time. Mars energy is impatient and very active. It is your Warrior Self who seeks to conquer new projects, who needs to release energy into the world in order to feel a sense of achievement. This stone requires you to undertake strenuous physical activity in order to release energy into it. Wear it in a leather pouch around your neck while you exercise, dance, enjoy sex, or have an exciting adventure of some kind. If you challenge someone's point of view, or engage in an argument, then make sure you take that energy home with you to release into your stone.

If you have been physically lazy, now is the time to take action and begin an exercise programme. Your vitality will increase greatly once you have released the tension that is locked between your shoulderblades and elsewhere in your body.

Mars in a stonecasting shows how you utilise this source of energy in your everyday life, and gives indication of your state of health, vitality and how you express yourself sexually.

The Key words for Mars are TENSION and ACTIVITY.

Stones of Mars

Stones which resonate to a Mars energy are Bloodstone, Ruby, Garnet, Carnelian and Tigerliron. The Mars stone should be a high energy one, which stimulates you and makes you feel more active.

My thoughts on Mars:

ENERGISING THE FIRST RING

The six stones of the First Ring can now be added to the Stone Pentacle. If you wish, you can use the ritual which appears at the end of the *Stone Pentacle* as a basis for binding these energies together.

Gather a bowl of rich earth and six candles (small slim votive candles are probably best — choose appropriate colours to be associated with the stones of the First Ring); place the stones of the Pentacle on the pattern, reaffirming the names and qualities of each stone, adding any changes which you have made in the process of working with those stones. Feel the strength of connection you now have with the stones and the understanding you have of how these energies work in your life.

Breathe deeply and evenly, centring your energy and making a strong connection with the stones of the First Ring as you pour them from hand to hand, feeling their vibrations. Now select each stone in turn and place it on the pattern, concentrating all your attention on the qualities of the stone. Pause to name each stone in the First Ring and light the appropriate votive candle. When you complete the pattern, sit quietly and meditate on the relationships between the Dreamstones. The Mandala below shows the pattern in which you should place the stones:

Mandala — The Stone Pentacle and First Ring

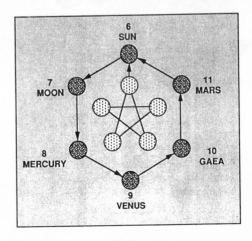

KEY ASSOCIATIONS

The Key associations for the stones of the First Ring are contained in the diagrams which appear at the beginning of each section. You will notice that some of the qualities mentioned are similar to those discussed in the Stone Pentacle; you will see that the Elemental Symbol appears in the top right-hand corner of the Key Word listings, which makes the relationship to the stones of the Pentacle clear. The strength and self-expression of the Sun amplifies an aspect of Fire, the energy of Mercury is a particular aspect of Air, and the Moon reflects the qualities of Water.

As we come to have a deeper understanding of the balance of forces in our lives, the dark and light contrast which we started with when casting the Yes, No and Question stones expands to incorporate the primary elements in the Stone Pentacle, then moves into more subtle arrangements with the Three Rings. In this way, the similarities between stones build patterns. Each of the planetary stones has a traditional association with one of the elemental energies. In the First Ring, these are as follows:

THE SUN	—	*FIRE*
THE MOON	—	*WATER*
MERCURY	—	*AIR*
VENUS	—	*EARTH*
GAEA	—	*EARTH*
MARS	—	*FIRE*

These Key Associations (often called 'correspondences') are qualities which expand, or amplify the meaning of a symbol. If, in a stonecasting, Mars and the Fire stone are in conjunction (only a stone's distance apart, or closer), then the Fire aspect is doubled. This can indicate extreme restlessness, impatience and an inability to discipline your energies. In similar manner, if the Moon stone and the Water stone are in conjunction, then you are probably being self-indulgent in emotional matters, and are more likely to be weepy, nostalgic or sensitive. These amplified meanings will largely depend on surrounding stones to aspect them for different situations.

If the Mars/Fire conjunction was closely aspected to, say, the Earth stone, this might indicate a containment of the fire, a discipline applied to it so that it can be used for creative projects. The Key Words for each stone can be added together to enable you to read meaning into the patterns. Mars/Tension + Fire/Energy was the set I used for the example above. Adding Earth/Practicality to it, lets you assume that a practical way of using this fire energy can be found. You would then look to the other stones surrounding these three to see where this energy could best be used.

The Associations for the First Ring are as follows:

☉ SUN △	☽ MOON ▽	☿ MERCURY △
CONSCIOUS SELF	DREAMING SELF	CHILD SELF
EXPRESSION	VISIONS	MIND
STRENGTH	SECRETS	PLAYFULNESS
CHARISMA	MEMORIES	TRAVEL
OPTIMISM	INTUITION	IDEAS
ACTIONS	MYSTERIES	MESSAGES
♀ VENUS △▽	⊕ GAEA ▽	♂ MARS △
COMPANION SELF	ANIMAL SELF	WARRIOR SELF
ART	NATURE	TENSION
HARMONY	HOME	VITALITY
ROMANCE	ENVIRONMENT	PROJECTS
DIPLOMACY	CONNECTION	ACTIVITY
CELEBRATIONS	RELAXATION	ADVENTURES

SAMPLE STONECASTING — PENTACLE & FIRST RING

You can see where the conjunctions occur in the following stonecasting. The Issue is to do with Fire, emphasised by the Sun being in conjunction with the Fire stone. Also in conjunction with the Spirit stone is Air (conjunct Earth), so this must also be taken into account regarding the main issue of the stonecasting, giving:

1 Spirit + Fire/sexuality/creativity + Sun/expression/strength

2 Spirit + Air/intellect/clarity + Earth/body/practicality/balance

99

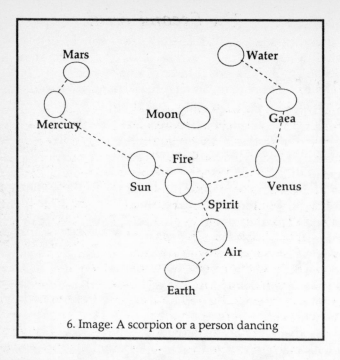

6. Image: A scorpion or a person dancing

The stones themselves (Sun, Fire, Spirit, Air, Earth) form a left-curved arc which is indicative of inner pathways, so the energy is likely turned inward, generating much personal creativity (fire) through positive expression (sun) of sexuality (fire) and a clear (air) understanding of the need to balance (earth) those energies so they do not override practical considerations. There are five stones in this configuration, so a creative resolution to tensions is indicated, though not without need for caution.

Other side issues should be read in a similar fashion, taking careful note of the conjunctions in the stonecasting and their relationship to other stones.

The Second Ring

JUPITER

Look to Jupiter for leadership, wealth, power and responsibility. It represents the first reaching for divine connection in the individual and the structures of religion, philosophy, meditation and the Higher Mind. Jupiter is the bright, laughing Self, gregarious and socially comfortable in a variety of different situations. This part of your Self is concerned with learning

and teaching, with justice and correct action. It is also a stone associated with good fortune of all kinds, so if it is well aspected in a reading (next to the random stone, for example) buying a lottery ticket is a very good idea.

The expansive nature of this stone shows what your position is in a social context, and is the planetary influence associated with actors, politicians and royalty. The extravagant enthusiasm which is typical of Jupiter links this stone to ideals of personal freedom and can, in some circumstances, indicate sexual promiscuity.

The ability to undertake a teaching profession is also indicated by this energy. Being the first stone of the Second Ring, it is here that we begin to deepen our interactions with others and accept responsibility for our own morality and personal honour. Jupiter is about expanding beyond the concerns of everyday and taking chances, living on the edge of uncertainty where new and positive things can happen. Examine where you fit into your social scene and make an effort to be helpful to your friends. Explore your own skills and be generous to others with your knowledge and energy. Concentrate on energising your Jupiter stone with the positive energy you are working with, and be open to new philosophies and patterns of behaviour. Record your changing perspectives in your journal.

The Key Words for Jupiter are EXPANSION and SOCIETY.

Stones of Jupiter

Stones which attract the possibilities of Jupiter are Amazonite, Lapis Lazuli, Sapphire, Turquoise, Chrysolite, Malachite and Jacinth.

My Thoughts on Jupiter:

SATURN

Carefully examine the limitations and restrictions in your life, the structure, organised systems and disciplines (or lack of them). Saturn is the Dark Self who is hidden from your full sight until you reach maturity. It is concerned with spiritual strength gained through isolation, and with the formation of your own ethical principles.

SATURN

ELDER SELF
CONTRACTION
DISCIPLINE
CONTAINMENT
AUTHORITY
CHALLENGES

Saturn is an energy associated with time — both in an abstract sense and the process of time in human lives — with maturity, ageing and, sometimes, senility. It is a stone which demands that you overcome self-imposed obstacles in order to reach your full potential. Saturn rules decisions, including business matters of all kinds. Saturnian people are serious and successful, not easily persuaded to take financial risks, and inclined to consider a situation fully before making up their minds. The Dark Self has the power to say 'no' to frivolous pursuits, over-indulgence or careless extravagance, especially when the timing is not right for such celebrations. On the physical plane, Saturn strives to define physical limits, sometimes to the detriment of health and energy resources; however, the Saturn aspect of your personality courts crises (in health, with authority figures or with philosophical ideas), for the tension that is released when an obstacle is overcome, or the lesson that is learned from the experience Saturn brings.

In a stonecasting, Saturn represents contained energy, self-control and your relationship with authorities, the social establishment, government and organisations of various kinds. It will indicate what structures are in place in your life and how you can challenge the boundaries which they represent. In a reading, Saturn also represents outside limiting forces, usually people who are older and wiser, and who are necessary to provide the controls and limitations to structure events in our lives until maturity enables us to work with and understand Saturn directly. The ability to work with, rather than against, limitations of life and make the most of learning experiences and challenges is associated with Saturn. It is the complementary pair to Jupiter and balances the expansiveness of that energy.

The Key Words for Saturn are DISCIPLINE and CHALLENGES.

Stones of Saturn

Stones which contain and control the power of Saturn are Jet, Onyx, Obsidian, Spinel, Ruby, Black Tiger's-Eye, Hematite and Polished Coal, all of a dark colour.

My Thoughts on Saturn:

URANUS

The energy of Uranus is eccentric and is typified by odd behaviour or bizarre interests. Rebels, activists and independent thinkers are strongly influenced by this energy, as are inventors and eccentrics of all kinds. Originality and the ability to make intuitive leaps, to think laterally, to be detached from emotional ties and pursue abstract concepts, are qualities associated with this stone.

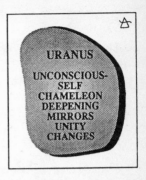

It is the first planetary energy which is not purely personal; rather, it is concerned with collective awareness and the pressures of collective or communal living. Uranus is disruptive and unbridled energy, driving you to confront your own individual skills and capitalise on your creative impulses.

Global consciousness and awareness of the range of collective knowledge is one aspect of this stone. The eccentric and often disruptive energy of this stone produces heretics, rebels and reformers, who are inspired to make changes in existing social orders. However, together with the inspiration of this stone comes an ability to understand underlying rhythms — of thought, of social identity, of metaphysical reality. Therefore, the position of this stone in a reading indicates the potential disruptions or creative resolutions which are being drawn into your life. This stone is strongly associated with radical changes to established patterns of thinking and behaviour, often manifesting in a violent or forceful manner. It signifies deep changes within the individual (and within society), and a deepening of understanding of the forces of the universe, particularly those of primeval, generative or creative natures. Its principle is one of unity, of gathering the scattered shards of splintered dreams to create a new whole.

The Key Words for Uranus are DEEPENING and CHANGES.

Stones of Uranus

Your Uranus stone should be one which has some particular peculiarity to it — an inclusion of another mineral, a flash of crystal, a streak of another colour — to represent the flash of inspiration that is attracted to this stone.

My Thoughts on Uranus:

NEPTUNE

Your stone for Neptune will be one which reawakens a sense of mythic reality, of fantasy (in its original sense), mysticism and a resonance with the poetic and bardic arts. Neptune is the storyteller and the weaver of myth, based in events in the world but made larger by their retelling. Neptune is associated with the primal sea, the archetypal energy which is an aspect of

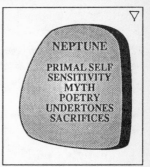

the ocean. Here is the realm of the collective unconscious, that sea of thought and memory which also contains our collective dreaming. The divinatory arts are most tied to the energy of Neptune, for it is most resonant with the reality of the Oracle. Poets interpret images from this place as much as do diviners and priests.

Astrologers associate Tethys (a Titan) with the planet Neptune, for the oceans were ruled first by Tethys before the time of Poseidon in Graeco-Roman myth. The energy of Neptune reminds us that history is a form of mythology, retold by the conquerors, and it needs a poet's vision to interpret the story of our ancestral voyages. A poet reads the undertones, the meaning between the lines, to see the portions of history which have been sacrificed in telling the ongoing tale. Likewise, a diviner interprets the underlying meaning of an Oracular device or system to see the personal history and unravelling tale of the individual.

Neptune is the Primal Self who instinctively understands that sometimes sacrifices are necessary in order to achieve dreams and, even though these are chosen by the individual, they are still painful ones. Sometimes it will be a choice to move to a different part of the world (leaving loved ones behind) and at other times it is the sacrifice of the storyteller (cutting away a well-loved piece of story for the benefit of the whole).

In working with Neptune, it is important to come to understand the power of poetry and myth. Read a poet of your choice, or a fairytale, a myth relating to your ancestral people or of the land in which you are now living. Make a deliberate attempt to see the mythology in history and notice how interpretations of history slant the events in a particular direction, changing the way in which they are read.

The Key Words for Neptune are MYTH and SENSITIVITY.

Stones of Neptune

Stones which awaken the sensitivity of Neptune are Amethyst, Beryl, Aquamarine and Lace Agate.

My Thoughts on Neptune:

PLUTO

Pluto is the Crone Self, the weaver in the dark reaches of our inner selves. This part of the Self knows the mysteries of death and rebirth and holds the thread of your life strand. It is the part of the self concerned with bindings — emotional, sexual, financial and political.

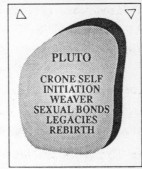

Look to this part of yourself for deep connections and attachments, for emotional intensity, examination of the occult mysteries and metaphysical reality and magic. Part of the hidden nature of Pluto is in the processes of regeneration — the body's immune and defense system (antibodies) — and, when this system breaks down, the transformation of death and rebirth. Pluto is concerned with other hidden forces in life as well, and is therefore associated with propaganda and power struggles, both ways of manipulating events and people.

Plutonian energy in a stonecasting can indicate both hidden forces and shared resources, for it is an energy which is concerned with community and society on the whole — with catastrophes, collective vision and action, both in a positive and negative sense. On a personal level, it is concerned with the deepest feelings, fears and possibilities for enlightenment possessed by the individual.

The Crone Self which is ruled by Pluto is concerned with initiation, with the transformation and regeneration which comes from catalytic experiences, confrontation with the meaning of death and rebirth. In Mystery Traditions, the process of initiation skirts the edge of dissolution of the individual psyche in order to effect the transformation which is brought by knowledge and personal connection with Deity. All initiatory experiences, whether in a formal or informal framework, partake of the nature of Pluto, for they sever you from the way you perceived reality before the experience — the Crone Self holds the blade which severs you from the innocence before knowledge is realised. Then, the hidden riches of Pluto may be explored.

The Key Words for Pluto are SEXUAL BONDS and INITIATION.

Stones of Pluto

Stones which resonate with the deep connections of Pluto are Obsidian, Black Pearl, Carbuncle, Snakestone (a kind of Agate) and Garnet.

My Thoughts on Pluto:

KARMA

Look to the Karma Stone for internal balance, for a sense of your place in the overall scheme of the universe. Each action you make spreads out from the locus of that moment in ripples, affecting things in far distant locations. Likewise, you are surrounded by the ripples and energy currents of other people's decisions in life.

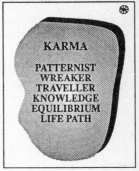

Karma is your principle of inner harmony, striving to achieve the best you are capable of in all endeavours, to act responsibly (knowing your actions have unseen results) and to find your own true Life Path. The Patternist Self (the part of the Self which recognises patterns and creates those of its own), and the Wreaker (who has the power to act on those patterns, changing their structure), make designs in both a deliberate and unconscious fashion, and are balanced by this stone. Karma is concerned with obligations and debts of energy incurred between people. One of its lessons is the equity which can be found when you neither give too much of yourself that you are diminished, nor take so much from others that you are overbalanced.

The Key Words for Karma are LIFE PATH and EQUILIBRIUM.

Stones of Karma

Stones which balance the energy of Karma should have some kind of directional quality to them (my own Karma stone is a Lapis Lazuli Pentagon which points in the direction of the Life Path in a stonecasting), and can be any kind of stone which you feel resonates with your own sense of personal equilibrium. Some choices here are Lapis Lazuli, Malachite, Agates of all kinds and Fossils.

My Thoughts on Karma:

ENERGISING THE SECOND RING

To energise the Second Ring and join it with the stones of the Pentacle and First Ring, gather a bowl of rich, dark earth and six new votive candles. Starting with the stones of the Pentacle, mark the Stone Pentacle on the earth and, with concentration, place each of the five stones in position. When you place each stone, name it and state its characteristics (either aloud or silently); imagine a line of connection forming between the stones.

Next, place the stones of the First Ring in position, again naming them and imagining the complex currents of energy which link the stones of this Ring with the Pentacle.

Finally, breathing deeply and evenly, centre your energies. Pour the stones of the Second Ring from hand to hand until you feel they are humming or vibrating with the energy of your deepest being. Place each stone on the Mandala (see below) and name it, with words like:

'I name this stone ...... and conjure the vibrations and
resonance of ...... into the Dreamstones and my life.'

Light a votive candle and place it in the earth beside that stone; continue until you have completed the stone mandala. Meditatively reflect on the qualities of each stone, cherishing them with your attention, feeling, seeing, perceiving the complex web of energies they create in your life. Allow the candles to burn until you have completed your meditation. Keep the candles and mark each one with the name of the stone with which it is associated; then you may burn the candle again whenever you feel it necessary to re-energise that stone.

MANDALA — STONE PENTACLE/FIRST & SECOND RINGS

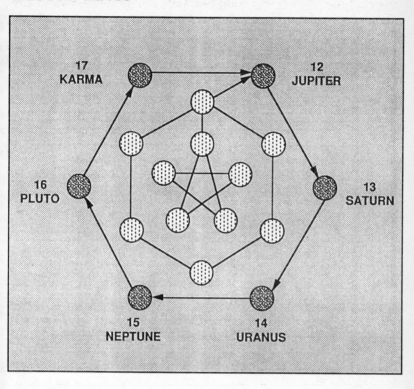

KEY ASSOCIATIONS

The Key Associations for the Second Ring are as follows:

113

♃ JUPITER △	♄ SATURN ▽	♅ URANUS △
BRIGHT SELF	ELDER SELF	UNCONSCIOUS SELF
EXPANSION	CONTRACTION	CHAMELEON
TEACHING	DISCIPLINE	DEEPENING
DRAMA	CONTAINMENT	MIRRORS
RITUAL	AUTHORITY	UNITY
SOCIETY	CHALLENGES	CHANGES
♆ NEPTUNE ▽	♇ PLUTO △▽	○ KARMA ✦
PRIMAL SELF	CRONE SELF	PATTERNIST
SENSITIVITY	INITIATION	WREAKER
MYTH	WEAVER	TRAVELLER
POETRY	SEXUAL BONDS	KNOWLEDGE
UNDERTONES	LEGACIES	EQUILIBRIUM
SACRIFICES	REBIRTH	LIFE PATH

The complexities of these stones allow you to make much more sensitive interpretations of the Dreamstone Oracle. The energy of Fire (energy) was expanded in the First Ring to incorporate the energies of the Sun (self-expression/strength) and Mars (tension/activity). In the Second Ring, subtleties emerge with Jupiter (expansion/teaching) which concentrates on the more social aspects of self-expression, together with the first mature reaching for the Fire of divine connection. Similarly, the energy of Water (feelings) in the Stone Pentacle deepened in the First Ring to embrace the energy of the Moon (visions/secrets); in the Second Ring, this principle deepens yet again with the stones of Neptune (dream/myth) and Pluto (initiation/transformation). In like manner, the energies of Earth and Air become evident in more complex forms in the stones of the Three Rings.

The increased number of stones means a geometric progression of possible meanings, and here your concentration on patterns in dreams, enhanced by practice with the Stone Pentacle and the First Ring, will be rewarded. By adding stones gradually, the complexity is not intimidating, because you have already acquired the necessary skills for interpreting pattern and are confident in the awareness of your own psychic and intuitive abilities.

The Third Ring

INTRODUCTION

The commentaries on the Third Ring are different from those on the First and Second Rings, as these regions of your Spirit are inherently beyond concrete description. Your reality is not mine; nor should I attempt to make absolutes of things which are very personal to you. In a stonecasting, the stones of the Third Ring are seen in context of a moment in time (whether you are interpreting for yourself or for another querent), in all its complexity. There are relationships between these stones and the stones of the Pentacle, First and Second Rings, which enhance their meaning.

In discussion of the Life Stone, for example, we look at the relationship between Fire and Earth (energy and the body), at the placement of the Mars stone (vitality, tension) and Saturn (restriction and containment). The placement of these stones in a casting allows you to make some assumptions about Life and Healing and how the ability to make changes to health is enhanced or restricted at a particular time.

With the God and Goddess Stone (they are nearly always read as a pair), we examine where they fall in a casting, what lies in conjunction with each, the patterns they are within (how many stones are in that pattern), and their relationship to both Sun/Moon (day and night) and Venus/Mars (the earlier polarisation of female and male energies in the individual).

LIFE

The Life Stone is the first stone of the Third Ring and represents your ability to manifest changes in the physical world through manipulation of energies. It is concerned with the Lifeforce, with containment of the etheric and subtle bodies within the envelop of your physical body. Your ability to effect healing within your own body and mind by spiritual disciplines, and

LIFE

HEALING SELF
NURTURING
PROTECTION
GENEROSITY
HEALTH
ASSISTANCE

to work with your own Lifeforce to heal others, is ruled by this stone. It is also called the Healing Stone because it relates to your vitality and nurturing ability — both of yourself and others.

Working with Life requires a commitment to principles of caring for health and emotional wellbeing. To begin to work consciously with this energy, do something supportive and caring for an acquaintance. It is easier to be caring about friends and family; however, that energy is more closely aspected to the Venus Stone. The Life Stone is concerned with an enlarged perspective of the world and the ability to make caring contacts with people you do not know well. The more complex vibrations of this stone make it one of service to community, though it concerns service through individual one-to-one contacts, rather than mass association. Bring your sense of life, of vitality and enthusiasm into other people's lives through optimism and generosity of spirit. You will know, within yourself, how best to express this unselfish, positive part of your personality.

The Key Words for Life are NURTURING and HEALING.

Stones of Life and Healing

Stones which are traditionally associated with healing are Quartz Crystal, Jade, Carnelian, Amethyst, Agate and unusual smooth beach stones.

My Thoughts on the Life Stone:

LOVE

The Love Stone is concerned with self-love, your relationship with your mother (from which all other relationships in your life proceed), with your ego and self-image as a lovable and loving human being. The Love stone is associated with the sense of self-worth which is necessary before you can relate to others in an equal fashion.

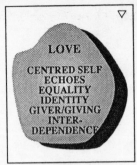

It is a deeper manifestation of relating which you explored with the Water Stone; and a more subtle and sensitive energy than that of Venus (the Companion Self). It is of a different order to the bonding and intensity of Pluto (the Crone Self), and is concerned with reaching for self-knowledge and identity as a platform from which to have a deep relationship with other whole beings. Interdependence is a Key Word for the Love Stone; it represents the gift, the giver and the recipient and the exchange of roles in changing circumstances. Dependence and independence, and the shift from the Mother Self to Child Self, and back again, provide the poles of experience and the tension necessary for manifestation of lasting changes in individual lives.

Its position in a stonecasting signifies how you are dealing with others — as a child or an adult, as an integrated entity or a fragmented one. It is a measure of personal integrity, self-knowledge and the ability to take criticism, to take advice or give of your own knowledge, experience and skills to others in close relationships, freely and without being diminished.

The Key Words for Love are INTERDEPENDENCE AND IDENTITY.

Stones of Love

Stones which are traditionally associated with Love are Diamonds, Rubies, all precious stones; however, semi-precious stones work just as well. I have found Rose Quartz, smooth beach stones and unusually marked pieces of Agate particularly effective as Stones of Love.

My Thoughts on Love:

MAGIC

The Magic Stone represents your ability to manipulate, and be manipulated by, the complex linkages with energies and forces in your life. It concerns the power to act and, more importantly, the power to refrain from doing so. It is concerned with system, and scientific method, yet also contains a sense of childlike wonder that the world is such a strange and mysterious place.

MAGIC

LINKING SELF
POWER
PROCESS
SYSTEMS
WONDER
POSSIBILITY

Magic is not so much a method of changing the world as it is a way of avoiding being changed by the world into something you are not. It is wonder, but also resilience, knowledge of your place in the overall scheme of things, and knowledge also that everything that happens does so in accordance with certain rules (even if you do not understand which ones govern a particular occurrence). It also deals with matters which are beyond the material or physical world, though actions taken in a Magical way will have manifestations and results in the real world.

In working with Magic, there is a balance between humour and seriousness, belief and disbelief (where you can hold two opposing ideas simultaneously). If ritual (associated with Mercury and Jupiter) can be expressed as 'theatre of the mind', then Magic could be called 'art of the psyche' — the changes we make in perception alter the way we act and react to events around us, often in subtle ways. There are many systems of Magic; however, the most basic kind resides in every human being — the ability to shape, to change, to alter your own reality in accordance with natural rhythms. You could view this book on the Dreamstones as a cookbook, containing basic information that will be changed by the Magic of your own perceptions, choice of ingredients and connection with the living Earth. Anything is possible, if you can only imagine it to be so.

The Key Words for Magic are POWER and POSSIBILITY.

Stones of Magic

Magic stones are those which stimulate powers of connection in you — they may be Fossils, pieces of Quartz with rainbows inside them, Silver-Sheen Obsidian, Opal Matrix, or any other stones which resonate with your own sense of magical perspective.

My Thoughts on Magic:

THE GOD STONE

The God Stone represents divine force, the primal fire of creativity, and the energy of the universe. The God Stone relates to public religion and questions of religious dogma; it is also the male self who resides within us all, whether as gender (if you are physically male), or as reflection and father.

The God Stone also relates to the primal Hunter who hearkens back to prehistory, and therefore represents survival of the species, protection and deep connection and identification with natural resources. The balance of the God is in taking from nature only that which is necessary for survival, so that the natural kingdom can be replenished. When this balance is not maintained, the aspect of the God who is wedded to chaos and the forces of Random energy, takes precedence and, like Pan in ancient Arcady or Dionysus in ancient Greece, unleashes the force of wildness, of panic and discord.

In his gentler aspects, He is the wind whispering through the grasses, the ripening grain, the clear sky and bright sunshine which warms and heals, and also the strength of the forest and the mysteries which live within its trees. The God is hunter and hunted, lover and beloved of the Earth, maker of music and strength of the Lifeforce seeking expression in creativity. He is power of the heavens, sky lord, protector and healer, wise old man, hermit, warrior and poet — he has as many aspects as there are people to identify those parts of themselves which resonate to a deeper energy of creation.

The Key Words for the God are FORCE and PRIMAL FIRE.

God Stones

God Stones are generally phallic-shaped, longer than they are round, though long triangular shapes also work very well. Stones with mixed minerals, representing the aspects of the God Force which are relevant to you, or those with interesting inclusions are also very suitable, as are Fossils, Petrified Wood, or Crystals.

My Thoughts on the God Stone:

THE GODDESS STONE

The Goddess Stone represents divine form, the primal Earth and generative principle, and the matter of the universe. The Goddess Stone relates to Earth rites and questions of religious connection (relinking); it is also the female self who resides within us all, whether as gender (if you are physically female) or as reflection and mother.

The Goddess Stone also relates to the Moon Maid, who changes her nature with the waxing and waning of the Moon. She is the primitive maid who becomes the mother, this process matched by the cycles of the moon in the sky. In prehistory, the darkness of the night was mysterious, with unknown dangers hiding in its shadows. The Moon triumphed over this darkness and silvered the land with Her light, making it less frightening. She is also a huntress by night, in stealth and in dreams, so her presence relates to finding your heart's desire and making a link with a sense of personal philosophy (found deep within the stillness of your own mind and body in the darkness and dreaming of night).

She, too, has a connection with Random energy, especially when creativity is not allowed to blossom within the individual, when art, poetry or celebration of life are stifled and become isolated from connection with the whole of human existence. The deep connection and relinking that is obvious in well-crafted tools, houses, clothing, food and art of all kinds is a celebration of the Goddess within. Where the God relates to taking that which is necessary for survival, the Goddess is the energy of 'making' from those basic ingredients something which is greater than the parts. Each is necessary to the other, just as yin and yang are necessary polarities in Taoist philosophy. They must be read together, with the individual standing at a point of balance between these different energies.

The Goddess is the fertile Earth which supports the ripening grain, the Muse who inspires poetry and art, the dance of

124

elements which creates life, and the cauldron or grail in which life is contained before birth. She is lover and beloved of the Hunter and Forest God, source of the Oracle, weaver, warrior, mother and crone. She has as many aspects as there are people to identify with the powers of formation.

The Key Words for the Goddess are RELINKING AND FORM.

Goddess Stones

Traditionally, Goddess Stones are ones with holes through the centre, or which are shaped like an equal-sided rounded triangle (shape of the womb), or like a heart. Any stone which matches your perceptions of the Goddess will be suitable. I have found that Amber, Coral, Agate, Gold Tiger's Eye, and worn river stones make good Goddess Stones.

My Thoughts on the Goddess Stone:

RANDOM

The Random Stone signifies those events which are inexplicable, unheralded and uncontrollable. This force is completely outside the ability of a human agency to change; the lesson of it is one of acceptance and survival.

The Random Stone is a floating variable which cannot be interpreted alone; it always relates to a particular stone or group of stones and indicates where the outside and uncertain forces are being experienced in a casting and in a querent's life. If the Random Stone falls in conjunction with the Saturn Stone, for example, you may assume the ordered elements in your life, or those areas of discipline, are very likely to be overturned or disrupted in ways impossible to guard against. The influence of the Random Stone must simply be accepted and lived with, making the best of the knowledge that plans are going to be disrupted in some way. This is sometimes a very positive thing — a combination of Jupiter (expansion), Fire (energy) and the Random Stone, for example, is extremely fortunate.

This Random energy is the power of wild magic, of Faerie, which is spoken of in most mythologies around the world. The influences of pookas, sprites, elves and wild Earth spirits are indicated by its position in a casting. It also represents the energy of the Earth's dreaming, in 'random' flashes of colour and influence; the oldest image for this is the Serpent.

The Key Words for the Random Stone are CHAOS and WILD MAGIC.

Random Stones

Your Random Stone can be a stone with two sides (indicating whether the Random force will be positive or negative in character) or one with distinctive marks and patterns on it — perhaps Opal Matrix, a Crystal with interesting inclusions, a polished river stone with a hollow on one side. It is important that the qualities of Random energy be represented on the stone itself, and that it is quite distinctly different from the other stones in your Dreamstone set.

My Thoughts on the Random Stone:

ENERGISING THE THIRD RING

Following the procedure given at the end of the First and Second Rings, gather the bowl of earth and a votive candle for each stone of the Third Ring. Place the stones of the Pentacle, First and Second Rings and, following the Mandala below, place each stone of the Third Ring in its appropriate position, naming the stone while you concentrate on its qualities; light the candles as you proceed.

Sit for a time in quiet meditation on the complex strands of energy which interconnect and weave between and within the Dreamstones. You should experience a real feeling of completion and connection with the energies of the living earth, with the mythic reality of the Dreamstones.

MANDALA — STONE PENTACLE & THREE RINGS

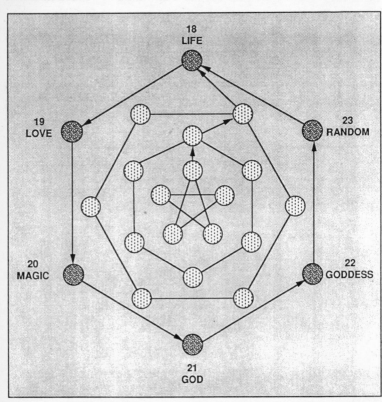

KEY ASSOCIATIONS

The Keys Associations for the Third Ring are as follows:

LIFE ▽△	LOVE ▽	MAGIC △
HEALING SELF	CENTRED SELF	LINKING SELF
NURTURING	ECHOES	POWER
PROTECTION	EQUALITY	PROCESS
GENEROSITY	IDENTITY	SYSTEMS
HEALTH	GIVER/GIVING	WONDER
ASSISTANCE	INTERDEPENDENCE	POSSIBILITY
GOD △✸△	**GODDESS ▽✸▽**	**RANDOM**
MALE SELF	FEMALE SELF	CHAOS
FORCE	FORM	SERPENT
PRIMAL FIRE	MATTER	WILD HUNT
PUBLIC RITES	EARTH RITES	LUCK
RELIGION	RELINKING	THE UNKNOWN
HUNTER	MOON MAID	WILD MAGIC

Professional Divination

Chapter 12
PROFESSIONAL DIVINATION

Ideally, professional diviners should be those people who have established a deep connection with their own psychic abilities, with the Oracle or with their own inner guides. There are many names for the Oracle, almost as many as practitioners, and a good diviner can use any device as a means to focus their ability; whether it is a formal system such as the Tarot, the Dreamstones or the I Ching, or a random pattern in the world around them, such as a drift of leaves, the flickering shapes of fire or, to be prosaic, a fall of paperclips in a crowded office.

The first thing you should do if you decide to become a professional diviner is to read a few basic texts on psychology and counselling. You will be in a care profession; there is no getting around the general assumption that if you are on the other side of a divinatory device, you are there to assist the person who comes to you as a querent — at the very least you are both entertainer and confidant(e). The second thing is to ascertain what the local laws are regarding professional divination. You will need to know where you stand on these matters, so that decisions can be made on a fee or donation for your services, your venue, and methods of advertising that you are available for consultations.

CROSSING THE PALM WITH SILVER

The often referred-to custom of crossing the palm of a diviner (or a gypsy in the original version of the saying) with silver, is not as superstitious as it may first appear. While there are varying opinions on whether divination should attract a fee, it is generally accepted that professional divination needs to address the issue of balance, and payment for advice is part of that balance. If, in your life, you continually do things for other people and do not receive a return, then you are burdening those people with unresolved obligations towards you; and they are incurring debts which they can ill afford. Similarly, if you constantly take from people without giving something back, you are incurring obligations yourself; again resulting in a lack of karmic balance. The gift of coin (particularly silver, as this has associations with the moon which influences divination), or an exchange of obligations by way of barter, balances the scales between diviner and querent and, indeed, between any two individuals who are undertaking any kind of transaction. Very few people will listen to advice for which they have not paid; the guilt which becomes associated with an unresolved obligation gets in the way. You may choose to work with barter, donations, exchanged favours or on a straight fee basis. The important principle is that something must be exchanged in order to restore the balance between individuals, so that they may relate to each other as equals.

WHO CONSULTS A PROFESSIONAL DIVINER?

Over a period of time, I have observed that people who seek formal divination from a professional fall into some basic categories, and they require different things from you. The following list is categorised according to the kind of divination they desire and some common explanations they give about why they have come to you. While not definitive, it does indicate the most common types of people who consult a professional diviner.

The Innocent

'I have never had a reading before. I was curious.' One of my favourite kinds of reading. This person is very open to new information, has not yet made up their mind but wants to know what it is about; they are prepared to be convinced that divination works. They need a running commentary on the form of divination you are using, its history and what kind of thing it can tell them. For example, casting stones differs from Tarot in that, while Tarot gives information on past/present/future in a precisely laid out pattern, stones create a pattern which can be interpreted to discover what the main issue is in a person's life right now — the underlying one about which they may not even be aware. This is derived from the stone closest to the Spirit Stone. The other stones give the balance of other events in their life, the surrounding areas which impact on them in particular ways. A stonecasting isolates a moment of time — the now — and makes assumptions about past and future from there.

The person's body language will be hesitant; yours should be certain. Meet their eyes, pitch your voice to be reassuring and watch for confirmation that you are on the right track with your interpretation by watching their unspoken language. Chances are that they will nod their head in confirmation quite unconsciously.

The Sceptic

'Tell me about myself.' This person sits back, folds their arms, assumes a blank face and tells you by their body language that they are not going to help you at all and that they fully expect that everything you say will be wrong.

It is interesting to note that sceptics do not realise how much they give away about themselves by their attitude, so if you are put off stride by their attitude, the first thing you can interpret is their body language. It is virtually impossible to interpret the Oracle for someone with whom you cannot make a connection. If you decide to persevere, asking a few general questions such as 'Have you ever been to a diviner before?', or 'What do you know about divination?', can begin to thaw them a little and give you an insight into their psyche through their voice. It is usually best either to make a connection before you begin casting the stones, or to have enough confidence to cast the stones and begin interpreting very quickly, on a first impression basis, until you sense some interaction happening. If you really have no ability to empathise with a person, you may choose to advise them that you are unable to obtain a reading from the Oracle for them, that this sometimes happens and is not a negative reflection on them, and then refer them to another diviner.

The Regular

'I need a reading to check that I'm making the right decision.' This person has certain stresses in their life right now and has chosen to seek divination in order to get a different perspective on what is happening. They are accustomed to visiting a diviner when their life takes a particular kind of turning, so will be quite comfortable and relaxed in consulting you. If it is the first time they have been to see you, there will be a short period of testing during which they establish that you know what you are doing (and are not a reader who keeps referring to their textbook every five minutes), before they settle down to receiving an interpretation of the forces that are operative in their lives at the time of the stonecasting. They do not want you to make decisions for them; simply to validate those decisions which they are making.

The Voyeur

'I thought it would be interesting.' This person probably does not believe that 'this fortune-telling nonsense' works, but wants to know what is going to happen to them anyway. They are basically there for entertainment. They may have been having a self-indulgent day shopping when, as an extra diversion, they have suddenly decided to treat themselves to a reading. If you are dressed in a colourful fashion, that is likely to be the reason why you have been chosen: your client may be feeling a little bored and in need of a lift. I have heard diviners say that they will not do an entertainment reading as they feel it does not treat their art seriously enough. This is really only a matter of personal taste.

Personally, I do not mind one of these readings at all. You can have fun over-emphasising your body language, with sweeping arm movements and graceful gestures and passes made with the hands. Draw their attention to the colours of the stones, to the patterns they make, to the reflections of light. Do not stop talking. For superficial interpretations like this, it can be useful to throw the stones several times, looking for different aspects of meaning. Tailor your language to suit the light-hearted nature of the reading and be very positive and optimistic. If you send someone away from a stonecasting feeling good about themselves then you have done something worthwhile. You can also insert useful information into the reading in the guise of being entertaining. There *is* a slight danger of making this kind of reading seem too trivial, thereby worrying people about whether all readers primarily work like this — take care to gauge the needs of your client and act accordingly.

The Patient

'I don't know what to do. Everything is a mess.' This person probably needs counselling, but would not think of going to a counsellor. If they visit a diviner, they can tell themselves that there is nothing seriously wrong with them. Visit a therapist and they are, by definition, not well. This is where your ability to listen carefully and lead the querent through their own decision-making process is of most use. The stones will provide you with an insight into the problem; it will require all your diplomacy and insight to gauge the language for interpretation. This person may try very hard to get you to make their decisions for them; resist the temptation and endeavour to have them sort the priorities you have seen into their own order, so that they can be led into making decisions for themselves. This person may need professional advice from a trained therapist — here, your knowledge of counselling and psychology will enable you to make an informed decision on whether to refer them to someone who specialises in this area.

The Victim

'It's not fair . . . why does everything have to happen to me?' This person needs a sympathetic ear and concrete common-sense advice, together with an interpretation of the Oracle which concentrates on practical and empowering actions which will result in a better self-image. Basic exercises for dealing with negative emotions are needed here. These may be as simple as advising them to meditate or say affirmations, to light specific coloured candles or take a long walk by the seaside, depending on what will work best for them; or they may be more complicated exercises which arise from your own magical experiences.

We all feel on occasion that life is all too much. Often the people who fall into this category are very capable in most areas of their lives, but have reached a crisis point where they need direction from outside themselves to know which way to turn their attention next. As a diviner, you will be able to see the overview of their lives at present and see which area can be brought into balance in the easiest and most direct fashion. Living in a high-technology environment can sometimes disconnect people from their own inner knowledge and common sense, and they become entangled in too many threads of thought to sort out the patterns for themselves. Your vision and empathy will assist them to find the skein which is least tangled, so that a start can be made in unravelling the problems in which they find themselves enmeshed.

Other people fit between these categories or may be in more than one at a time. There is nothing to stop someone who is going through a period of extreme anxiety (the Patient) from finding entertainment (the Voyeur) and the release of laughter in consulting a diviner. At the very least, you will be entertaining and your querents will go away with a positive outlook on the situations which are currently occurring in their life. At best, you can interpret the Oracle in such a way that a person will hear exactly the words which make their situation more clear. It is not at all uncommon for someone to go to a diviner because they want help in 'thinking out loud', or need validation of the things which they perceive are happening in their lives, a reassurance from an experienced psychic that they are not imagining things, or over-reacting to events around them.

Part IV
VARIATIONS
AND RESOURCES

Chapter 13
DREAMSTONES

The number of stones you cast is limited only by the ability to cup them in the palm of one hand — usually twenty-five will be the maximum number. However, this does not prevent you from having a selection of basic stones that exceeds twenty-five, enabling you to choose which ones you will interpret for a given situation. A friend has over thirty stones in her Dreamstone set, but would interpret fewer than twenty in a casting. There are various ways of deciding which stones to use, among which are the following:

1 Display your Dreamstones in a bowl and allow a querent to select a set number of them for interpretation. If you are interpreting the stones for yourself, close your eyes and select them randomly.

2 Separate your stones into those which apply to everyday situations and those that relate to more esoteric or complex areas of the human spirit; then you can select the appropriate stones for a particular querent.

3 Gather all your stones in cupped hands and, in a preliminary casting, scatter them onto a specially prepared casting cloth, one with a defined pattern in the centre. The stones which fall within the defined pattern are those which you will gather and interpret for a casting of the Dreamstones. The stones which fall outside the pattern should be gathered up and returned to their storage container.

Sample Casting Cloth

STONES FOR YOUR DREAMS

Each person's vision of the Oracle is individual and uniquely personal, so the stones in your set will eventually diverge from the Dreamstones described in this book. The following examples show some possible changes made by myself and a couple of other Dreamstone diviners:

The Moon

This stone is separated into stones representing the phases of the Moon, or the aspects of the Goddess who relates to those phases. This variation is particular to folk whose philosophical beliefs lead them to work with these energies. The separate stones are:

140

MAIDEN: Innocence, a willingness to begin a new cycle, increasing energy.

MOTHER: Knowledge, an ability to live with necessary decisions, peak of energy.

CRONE: Maturity, an ability to let go of things in life which are no longer needed, decreasing energy, used wisely.

MYSTERY: Hidden Truths, an ability to perceive and experience the ineffable.

The Dream Stone

This is a variation of my own which represents the voice of the Oracle as it speaks to you in your dreams. The position of this stone, together with the placement of the Moon and Neptune stones, gives a clear indication of the power and focus of your hidden dreams. It allows you to see which area of your life is most strongly affected by your deepest dreaming. It is added to the Dreamstones when interpreting professionally, or can be added to the Stone Pentacle to give a deeper understanding of the influence of elemental energies.

The Career Stone

This stone more specifically deals with job prospects, career goals and employment-oriented activities — otherwise this information can be gleaned from the position of Mars (activity), Earth (work, physical endeavour, practicality) and Saturn (authority, finances, organisation).

Season Stones

These stones amplify the meanings of the elemental stones and separate this aspect of the four elements. The reason for this separation is to give information on patterns of energy at different times of the year; you derive this from the stones which surround each of the Season Stones. Their other meanings are:

SPRING: Activity, awareness, undertaking
new projects, travel plans, changes.

SUMMER: Energy, creative social contacts,
making the most of opportunities.

AUTUMN: Consolidating efforts made in
previous seasons, a time of work,
ongoing social commitments,
gathering information for the time
of reflection to come.

WINTER: Reflection, solitude, inner peace,
study, personal projects, long nights
and short days.

The Time Stone

A stone which relates to perceptions such as space/time relationships, a sense of timing (actions taken at precisely the right moment), duration of particular events (see surrounding stones) and a sense of history and tradition.

SYSTEMS OF CASTING

Other possibilities for Dreamstones are to name your stones for the Deities in a particular mythological system. For example, Norse casting stones could consist of eighteen stones (six Aesir, six Vanir, six Other), with meanings of the stones derived from the attributes of those Deities and other beings (Giants, Dwarves, etc.) contained within that mythos. In Nordic mythology there are two major tribes of Deities: the Aesir, an up-and-coming, rather male-oriented group of warriors and adventurers; and the Vanir, survivors of an older Earth Religion.

The Stones of Brisingamen

A few years ago, I gave a set of casting stones to a friend, Bill Beattie, who had been attracted by the simplicity of the Dreamstones. He set about trying to pick up the art, but found an obstacle in the attributions given to the stones. He decided that if the system was not working for him, then he should personalise it and transform it to better suit his requirements. He needed a homogenous system in a mythic language he could easily click into. The solution he settled on was (his word) 'Scandinavianisation'.

Nordic mythology had long been a favourite of his, though runework was not his particular horn of mead, but by combining Norse mythology with stone casting, he felt as if he might make some progress with both studies. I asked him to describe his method for creating his own Dreamstone casting set:

'The first step was not to find mythic characters to fit each stone, but to list which figures most required representation in the revised collection. Having made this list, I tallied the participants and found myself still at the magic number eighteen, the same as my initial set (stones for the Three Rings). The number seemed auspicious under the circumstances: nine frequently crops up in the Eddas as a particularly potent number (notably, in the nine worlds), while eighteen has especial oracular significance, being the number of runes won by Odin during his self-sacrificial shamanic quest on the world tree, Yggdrasill. Of these eighteen stones, three groupings emerged: nine Aesir Stones, four Vanir, and five from Other Branches.

Then came the re-allocation of the existing stones. Some made a fairly effortless transition: in the case of the former Sun Stone, a piece of quartz crystal became retitled Baldr's Stone. Others took on quite new characteristics; some had to be replaced with pieces better suited to the nature of particular Deities.

On casting this new set, a change was immediately apparent. The stones no longer represented various qualities and potentialities. They were people, quite familiar to me, gathered together in communion, collaboration, confrontation or questing. Their dance, revealed through the patterns of the stones, began to accurately delineate the play of my own inner energies and travelling. The techniques by which these patterns may be interpreted are the same as Rhea has described elsewhere.' (For a full interpretation of the Brisingamen Stones, see Appendix B.)

YOUR OWN MYTHIC SYSTEM

Other possibilities for exploration of mythic systems are:

Celtic — Cretan — Amer-Indian — Welsh — Indian — Chinese — Greek — African

The range is virtually endless. The background in stonecasting provided by this book should enable you to feel confident in altering the stones to suit both your own personality and your philosophical approach.

PEOPLE STONES

Your Dreamstones can be used to examine the relationships between people in a group, much as Bill (in the Brisingamen Stones) found that the stones related to each other like people. The way this is done is to designate a stone to each person, with extra stones representing the goals, plans or areas of concern of that group. Have each person take their stone and concentrate their energy on it before casting them in the usual manner. Ask the question: 'What is the pattern of energy for this group at the moment?' and cast the stones. Interpret the relationship between stones as if it were the relationship between the people, and get everyone in a group to participate in interpreting the connections.

Some basic guidelines for using the Dreamstones as People Stones are as follows:

☆ **One stone alone**   Someone who is feeling isolated, or who chooses to be isolated from all the activities of a group.

☆ **Two stones together**   A partnership or close association.

☆ **Three stones together**   The nucleus of a sub-group, but tensions can develop if everyone is not getting an equal say. A good pattern for creative ideas. Check to see if any of these three forms relationships with other stones.

☆ **Four stones together**   Is it a balanced square pattern (which indicates stability, and possibly stubbornness), or a rhomboid shape (which adds flexibility to the stability)?

☆ **Five stones together**   Creative resolution of difficulties or disharmony caused by everyone wanting to go off in their own direction; a grouping of five stones always denotes tension, and the colours of the stones (and their usual meanings) will give you information on whether the tension is positive or not.

☆ **Curved Patterns**   Curved patterns indicate flexibility, so the group of people is able to change and grow with each other. Look to see which stone is at the base of a curve or spiral, as this is likely to be the person who begins new projects.

☆ **Angular Patterns/Straight Lines**   Angular patterns and straight lines indicate purpose, drive and determination (though sometimes at the expense of creative solutions and innovation). The person at the end of a straight line is the one whose sense of direction is an obvious influence on the group.

☆ **Centre of the Stonecasting**   A person (or rather the stone they have chosen!) which falls at the very centre of a reading is an anchor point for the group, someone who is literally at the centre of the group's concerns.

Proximity of, or distance between, stones will indicate the same thing in real life, and when you take into account the normal meaning of the stones, this will add information to your reading. For example, if the stones are chosen at random and with eyes closed, you can ask that people choose a stone which feels 'right' to them. If this were a stone such as the Mars Stone, and it fell in close proximity to the Fire Stone or the Sun Stone, you could assume that sparks are going to fly between the people who chose these stones. This could be a sexual attraction or creative teamwork if positively aspected in the midst of circular or curved patterns, but could indicate rivalry and antagonism if surrounded by angular patterns.

Using stones as People Stones is a good introduction to stonecasting for those who have never encountered it before, and is a technique I have often used in workshops on the Dreamstones. It very quickly breaks down barriers between people who do not know each other, and allows everyone to have some first-hand experience at interpreting patterns in a stonecasting. For people who have done work together as a group for some time, it can provide a new insight into the existing relationships within the group.

145

Key Associations

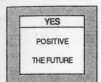

YES

POSITIVE

THE FUTURE

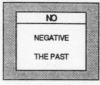

NO

NEGATIVE

THE PAST

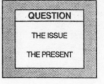

QUESTION

THE ISSUE

THE PRESENT

EARTH

LAND SELF
BODY
PRACTICALITY
BALANCE
BONES

WATER

SEA SELF
FEELINGS
EMOTIONS
RELATING
FLUIDS

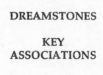

DREAMSTONES

**KEY
ASSOCIATIONS**

FIRE

FIRE SELF
WILL
SEXUALITY
CREATIVITY
ENERGY

AIR

TALKING SELF
INTELLECT
MIND
CLARITY
BREATH

SPIRIT

HIGHER SELF
RADIANCE
INTEGRATION
SYNTHESIS
SOUL

SUN

CONSCIOUS SELF
EXPRESSION
STRENGTH
CHARISMA
OPTIMISM
ACTIONS

MOON

DREAMING SELF
VISIONS
SECRETS
MEMORIES
INTUITION
MYSTERIES

MERCURY

CHILD SELF
MIND
PLAYFULNESS
TRAVEL
IDEAS
MESSAGES

VENUS

COMPANION SELF
ART
HARMONY
ROMANCE
DIPLOMACY
CELEBRATIONS

GAEA

ANIMAL SELF
NATURE
HOME
ENVIRONMENT
CONNECTION
RELAXATION

MARS

WARRIOR SELF
TENSION
VITALITY
PROJECTS
ACTIVITY
ADVENTURES

Key Associations

JUPITER	SATURN	URANUS
BRIGHT SELF	ELDER SELF	UNCONSCIOUS SELF
EXPANSION	CONTRACTION	CHAMELEON
TEACHING	DISCIPLINE	DEEPENING
DRAMA	CONTAINMENT	MIRRORS
RITUAL	AUTHORITY	UNITY
SOCIETY	CHALLENGES	CHANGES

NEPTUNE	PLUTO	KARMA
PRIMAL SELF	CRONE SELF	PATTERNIST
SENSITIVITY	INITIATION	WREAKER
MYTH	WEAVER	TRAVELLER
POETRY	SEXUAL BONDS	KNOWLEDGE
UNDERTONES	LEGACIES	EQUILIBRIUM
SACRIFICES	REBIRTH	LIFE PATH

LIFE	LOVE	MAGIC
HEALING SELF	CENTRED SELF	LINKING SELF
NURTURING	ECHOES	POWER
PROTECTION	EQUALITY	PROCESS
GENEROSITY	IDENTITY	SYSTEMS
HEALTH	GIVER/GIVING	WONDER
ASSISTANCE	INTERDEPENDENCE	POSSIBILITY

GOD	GODDESS	RANDOM
MALE SELF	FEMALE SELF	CHAOS
FORCE	FORM	SERPENT
PRIMAL FIRE	MATTER	WILD HUNT
PUBLIC RITES	EARTH RITES	LUCK
RELIGION	RELINKING	THE UNKNOWN
HUNTER	MOON MAID	WILD MAGIC

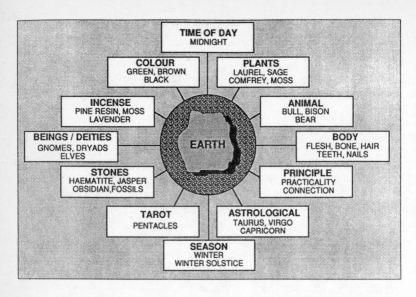

TIME OF DAY
MIDNIGHT

COLOUR
GREEN, BROWN
BLACK

PLANTS
LAUREL, SAGE
COMFREY, MOSS

INCENSE
PINE RESIN, MOSS
LAVENDER

ANIMAL
BULL, BISON
BEAR

BEINGS / DEITIES
GNOMES, DRYADS
ELVES

EARTH

BODY
FLESH, BONE, HAIR
TEETH, NAILS

STONES
HAEMATITE, JASPER
OBSIDIAN, FOSSILS

PRINCIPLE
PRACTICALITY
CONNECTION

TAROT
PENTACLES

ASTROLOGICAL
TAURUS, VIRGO
CAPRICORN

SEASON
WINTER
WINTER SOLSTICE

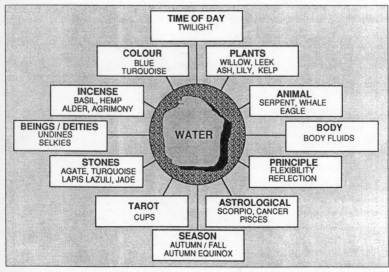

TIME OF DAY
TWILIGHT

COLOUR
BLUE
TURQUOISE

PLANTS
WILLOW, LEEK
ASH, LILY, KELP

INCENSE
BASIL, HEMP
ALDER, AGRIMONY

ANIMAL
SERPENT, WHALE
EAGLE

BEINGS / DEITIES
UNDINES
SELKIES

WATER

BODY
BODY FLUIDS

STONES
AGATE, TURQUOISE
LAPIS LAZULI, JADE

PRINCIPLE
FLEXIBILITY
REFLECTION

TAROT
CUPS

ASTROLOGICAL
SCORPIO, CANCER
PISCES

SEASON
AUTUMN / FALL
AUTUMN EQUINOX

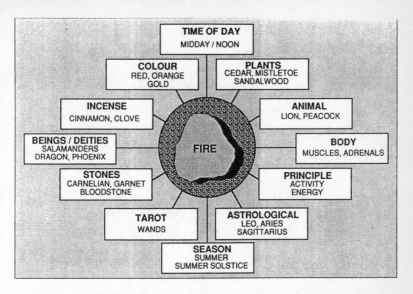

TIME OF DAY
MIDDAY / NOON

COLOUR
RED, ORANGE
GOLD

PLANTS
CEDAR, MISTLETOE
SANDALWOOD

INCENSE
CINNAMON, CLOVE

ANIMAL
LION, PEACOCK

BEINGS / DEITIES
SALAMANDERS
DRAGON, PHOENIX

FIRE

BODY
MUSCLES, ADRENALS

STONES
CARNELIAN, GARNET
BLOODSTONE

PRINCIPLE
ACTIVITY
ENERGY

TAROT
WANDS

ASTROLOGICAL
LEO, ARIES
SAGITTARIUS

SEASON
SUMMER
SUMMER SOLSTICE

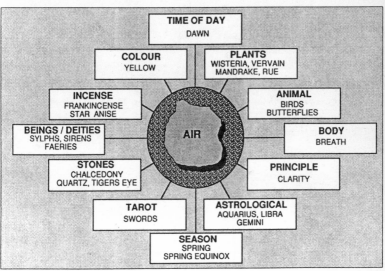

TIME OF DAY
DAWN

COLOUR
YELLOW

PLANTS
WISTERIA, VERVAIN
MANDRAKE, RUE

INCENSE
FRANKINCENSE
STAR ANISE

ANIMAL
BIRDS
BUTTERFLIES

BEINGS / DEITIES
SYLPHS, SIRENS
FAERIES

AIR

BODY
BREATH

STONES
CHALCEDONY
QUARTZ, TIGERS EYE

PRINCIPLE
CLARITY

TAROT
SWORDS

ASTROLOGICAL
AQUARIUS, LIBRA
GEMINI

SEASON
SPRING
SPRING EQUINOX

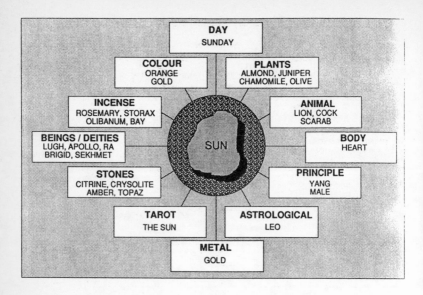

DAY
SUNDAY

COLOUR
ORANGE
GOLD

PLANTS
ALMOND, JUNIPER
CHAMOMILE, OLIVE

INCENSE
ROSEMARY, STORAX
OLIBANUM, BAY

ANIMAL
LION, COCK
SCARAB

BEINGS / DEITIES
LUGH, APOLLO, RA
BRIGID, SEKHMET

SUN

BODY
HEART

STONES
CITRINE, CRYSOLITE
AMBER, TOPAZ

PRINCIPLE
YANG
MALE

TAROT
THE SUN

ASTROLOGICAL
LEO

METAL
GOLD

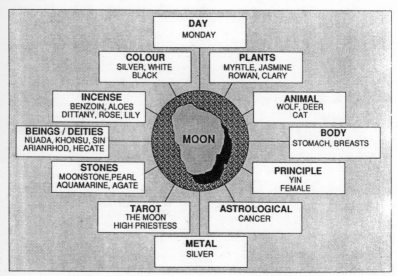

DAY
MONDAY

COLOUR
SILVER, WHITE
BLACK

PLANTS
MYRTLE, JASMINE
ROWAN, CLARY

INCENSE
BENZOIN, ALOES
DITTANY, ROSE, LILY

ANIMAL
WOLF, DEER
CAT

BEINGS / DEITIES
NUADA, KHONSU, SIN
ARIANRHOD, HECATE

MOON

BODY
STOMACH, BREASTS

STONES
MOONSTONE, PEARL
AQUAMARINE, AGATE

PRINCIPLE
YIN
FEMALE

TAROT
THE MOON
HIGH PRIESTESS

ASTROLOGICAL
CANCER

METAL
SILVER

Key Associations

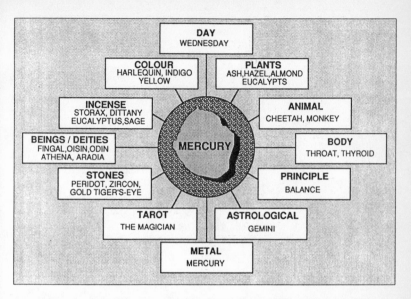

DAY WEDNESDAY

COLOUR HARLEQUIN, INDIGO YELLOW

PLANTS ASH, HAZEL, ALMOND EUCALYPTS

INCENSE STORAX, DITTANY EUCALYPTUS, SAGE

ANIMAL CHEETAH, MONKEY

BEINGS / DEITIES FINGAL, OISIN, ODIN ATHENA, ARADIA

MERCURY

BODY THROAT, THYROID

STONES PERIDOT, ZIRCON, GOLD TIGER'S-EYE

PRINCIPLE BALANCE

TAROT THE MAGICIAN

ASTROLOGICAL GEMINI

METAL MERCURY

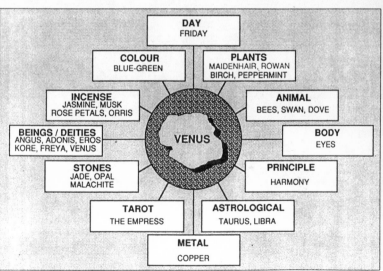

DAY FRIDAY

COLOUR BLUE-GREEN

PLANTS MAIDENHAIR, ROWAN BIRCH, PEPPERMINT

INCENSE JASMINE, MUSK ROSE PETALS, ORRIS

ANIMAL BEES, SWAN, DOVE

BEINGS / DEITIES ANGUS, ADONIS, EROS KORE, FREYA, VENUS

VENUS

BODY EYES

STONES JADE, OPAL MALACHITE

PRINCIPLE HARMONY

TAROT THE EMPRESS

ASTROLOGICAL TAURUS, LIBRA

METAL COPPER

151

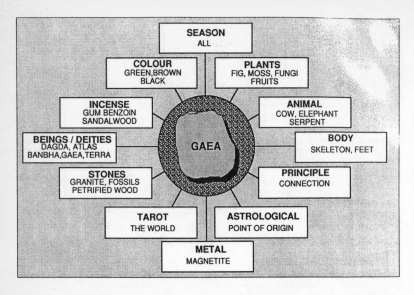

SEASON
ALL

COLOUR
GREEN, BROWN
BLACK

PLANTS
FIG, MOSS, FUNGI
FRUITS

INCENSE
GUM BENZOIN
SANDALWOOD

ANIMAL
COW, ELEPHANT
SERPENT

BEINGS / DEITIES
DAGDA, ATLAS
BANBHA, GAEA, TERRA

GAEA

BODY
SKELETON, FEET

STONES
GRANITE, FOSSILS
PETRIFIED WOOD

PRINCIPLE
CONNECTION

TAROT
THE WORLD

ASTROLOGICAL
POINT OF ORIGIN

METAL
MAGNETITE

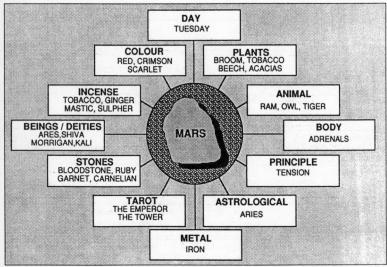

DAY
TUESDAY

COLOUR
RED, CRIMSON
SCARLET

PLANTS
BROOM, TOBACCO
BEECH, ACACIAS

INCENSE
TOBACCO, GINGER
MASTIC, SULPHER

ANIMAL
RAM, OWL, TIGER

BEINGS / DEITIES
ARES, SHIVA
MORRIGAN, KALI

MARS

BODY
ADRENALS

STONES
BLOODSTONE, RUBY
GARNET, CARNELIAN

PRINCIPLE
TENSION

TAROT
THE EMPEROR
THE TOWER

ASTROLOGICAL
ARIES

METAL
IRON

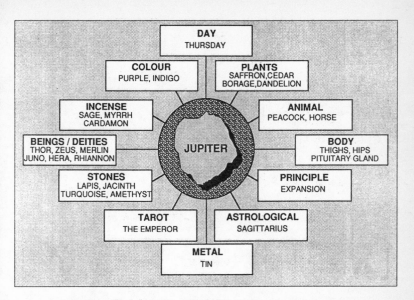

DAY
THURSDAY

COLOUR
PURPLE, INDIGO

PLANTS
SAFFRON, CEDAR
BORAGE, DANDELION

INCENSE
SAGE, MYRRH
CARDAMON

ANIMAL
PEACOCK, HORSE

BEINGS / DEITIES
THOR, ZEUS, MERLIN
JUNO, HERA, RHIANNON

JUPITER

BODY
THIGHS, HIPS
PITUITARY GLAND

STONES
LAPIS, JACINTH
TURQUOISE, AMETHYST

PRINCIPLE
EXPANSION

TAROT
THE EMPEROR

ASTROLOGICAL
SAGITTARIUS

METAL
TIN

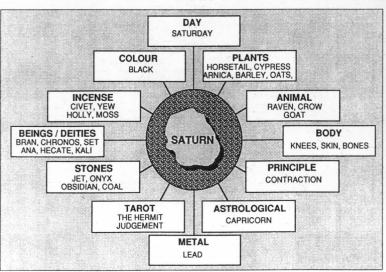

DAY
SATURDAY

COLOUR
BLACK

PLANTS
HORSETAIL, CYPRESS
ARNICA, BARLEY, OATS,

INCENSE
CIVET, YEW
HOLLY, MOSS

ANIMAL
RAVEN, CROW
GOAT

BEINGS / DEITIES
BRAN, CHRONOS, SET
ANA, HECATE, KALI

SATURN

BODY
KNEES, SKIN, BONES

STONES
JET, ONYX
OBSIDIAN, COAL

PRINCIPLE
CONTRACTION

TAROT
THE HERMIT
JUDGEMENT

ASTROLOGICAL
CAPRICORN

METAL
LEAD

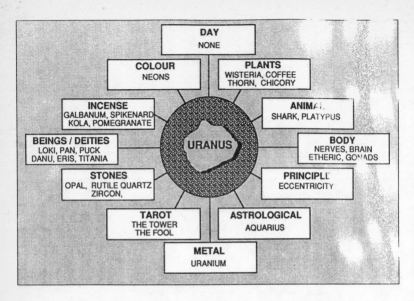

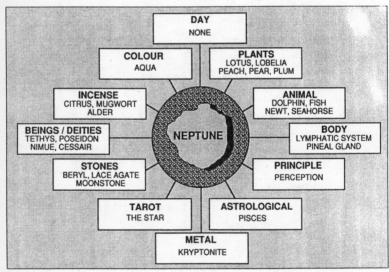

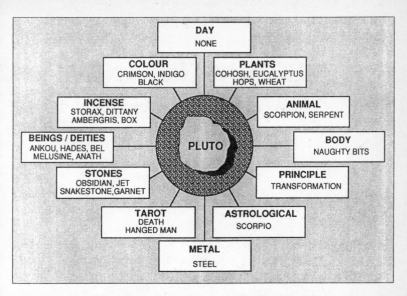

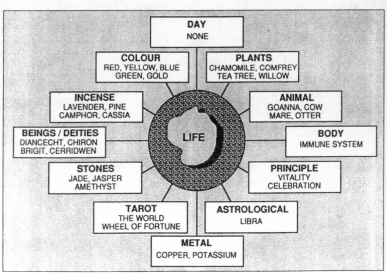

155

RESOURCES AND SAMPLE PAGES

RESOURCES
Australia
Stones

DREAMSTONES P O Box 1030, Canberra A.C.T. 2601
For Dreamstone casting sets and leather stone bags. International mail order. Send s.a.e. for brochure and price list.

MYSTERYS 386 Darling Street, Balmain, N.S.W. 2041
For sets of ten initial casting stones and additional stones by mail order (International).

CASTING CLOTHS Dreamstones, as above.
Send s.a.e. for brochure.

CONTACTS Shadowplay, P O Box 343, Petersham, N.S.W. 2049
Quarterly publication. Editors: Rhea Loader and Bill Beattie.

England

MYSTERIES 9-11 Monmouth Street, Covent Garden, London WC2H 9DA.

USA

STONES AND CASTING CLOTHS 'Mythos', PO Box 21768, Wa. 98111-3768. Send s.a.e. for catalogue. Contact: Rhea Loader.

A DREAM JOURNAL

DATE   SEASON

MOON PHASE   DAY OF CYCLE

FEELINGS...

IMAGES & IDEAS

SIGNIFICANT PATTERNS & INTERPRETATIONS

PAGE #

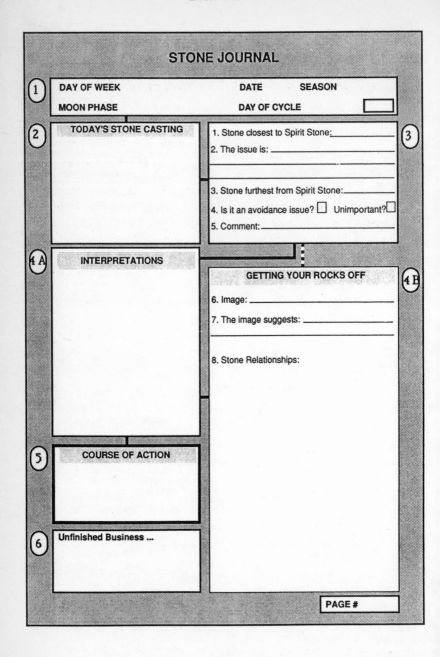

BIBLIOGRAPHY
AND FURTHER READING

Adler, M. *Drawing Down the Moon: Witches, Druids, Goddess-Worshippers, and Other Pagans in America Today* Mass. USA: Beacon Press, 1986.

Agrippa, H.C. *The Philosophy of Natural Magic* Antwerp, 1531. Reprint USA: University Books, 1974.

Anderson, N. *Numerology: The Secret Power of Numbers* NY, USA: Samuel Weiser Inc., 1979.

Anon. *The Complete Book of Fortune* London 1936. Reprint UK: Chatto & Windus Ltd, 1988.

Babcock, W. *Jung, Hesse, Harold: A Spiritual Psychology* NY, USA: The Harold Institute, 1983.

Beyerl, P. *The Master Book of Herbalism* WA, USA: Phoenix Publishing Inc., 1984.

Blake, W. *The Portable Blake* (Ed. Alfred Kazin) USA: Penguin Books,1979.

Blakeley, J.D. *The Mystical Tower of the Tarot* London, UK: Robinson & Watkins Books Ltd, 1974.

Blum, R. *The Book of Runes* Sydney, Australia: Angus & Robertson, 1984.

Bonewitz, P.E.I. *Real Magic: An Introductory Treatise on the Basic Principles of Yellow Magic* London, UK: Open Gate Books with Macmillan London Ltd, 1972.

Bonewitz, R. *Cosmic Crystals: Crystal Consciousness and the New Age* Wellingborough, UK: Turnstone Press Ltd, 1984.

Bradley, R. *Dragonshadow* Sydney, Australia: Women's Redress Press Inc., 1989.

Buckland, R. *Secrets of Gypsy Fortunetelling* Minneapolis, USA: Llewellyn Publications, 1988.

Campbell, J. & Roberts, R. *Tarot Revelations* CA, USA: Vernal Equinox Press, 1982.

Crow, W.B. *Precious Stones: Their Occult Power and Hidden Significance* UK: The Aquarian Press, 1970.

Cunningham, S. *Cunningham's Encyclopedia of Crystal, Gem & Metal Magic* USA: Llewellyn Publications, 1988.

Doczi, G. *The Power of Limits* Colorado, USA: Shambhala Publications Inc., 1981.

Drury, N. *Vision-Quest: A Personal Journey Through Magic and Shamanism* Dorset, UK: Prism Press, 1984.

Fernie, W.T. *The Occult And Curative Powers of Precious Stones* San Francisco, USA: Harper & Row, 1981.

Gawain, S. *Creative Visualisation* NY, USA: Bantam Books, 1982.

Graves, R. *Greek Myths* London, UK: Cassel & Co. Ltd, 1965.

Graves, R. *The White Goddess* London, UK: Faber & Faber, 1977.

Gray, W.G. *The Rite of Light: A Mass of the Western Inner Mystery Tradition* Cheltenham, UK: privately printed, 1976.

Greene, L. *The Astrology of Fate* London, UK: George Allen & Unwin Ltd, 1984.

Guthrie, W.K.C. *The Greeks and Their Gods* Boston, USA: Beacon Press, 1955.

Harding, M.E. *Psychic Energy: Its source and transformation* Princeton University Press, 1973.

Howard, M. *The Magic of the Runes: Their Origins and Occult Power* NY, USA: Samual Weiser Inc., 1977.

Howard, M. *The Runes and Other Magical Alphabets* UK: The Aquarian Press, 1984.

Hunger, R. *The Magic of Amber* London, UK: NAG Press Ltd, 1977.

Jacobs, J. (Ed) *Celtic Fairy Tales* NY, USA: Dover Publications Inc., 1892. Reprint 1968.

Jung, C.G. *Psychology and the Occult* Princeton, USA: Princeton University Press, 1977.

Jung, C.G. *Psychology and Alchemy* Princeton, USA: Princeton University Press, 1980.

Katzeff, P. *Full Moons: Fact and Fantasy about Lunar Influence* NJ, USA: Citadel Press, 1981.

King, X.F. *The Encyclopedia of Fortune-Telling* London, UK: Octopus Books, 1988.

Kozminsky, I. *Numbers: Their Meaning and Magic* NY, USA: Samuel Weiser Inc., 1912. Reprint 1980.

Kunz, G.F. *The Mystical Lore of Precious Stones* Vols 1 & 2. CA, USA: Newcastle Publishing Co. Inc., 1913, 1915. Reprint 1986.

Leland, C.G. *Etruscan Magic and Occult Remedies* NY, USA: University Books, 1963.

Lewis, I.M. *Ecstatic Religion: An Anthropological Study of Spirit Possession and Shamanism* Middlesex, UK: Penguin Books Ltd, 1971.

Line, D. & J. *Fortune-Telling by Runes* UK: The Aquarian Press, 1984.

Malaclypse the Younger, *Principia Discordia: or, How I found Goddess and what I did to Her when I found Her* WA, USA: Loompanics Unlimited, 4th Ed.

Mann, A.T. *The Round Art: The Astrology of Time and Space* UK: Dragon's World Ltd, 1979.

Markale, J. *Women of the Celts* Rochester, USA: Inner Traditions International, Ltd, 1986.

Medici, M. *Good Magic* London, UK: Macmillan Ltd, 1988.

Meyer, F. S. *Handbook of Ornament* NY, 1892, USA: Dover Publications Inc., 1957.

Neumann, E. *The Origins and History of Consciousness* Princeton, USA: Princeton University Press, 1973.

Osborn, M. *Rune Games* UK: Routledge & Kegan Paul Ltd, 1982.

Paulsen, K. *The Complete Book of Magic and Witchcraft* NY, USA: Signet, 1971.

Pavitt, W. *The Book of Talismans, Amulets & Zodiacal Gems* CA, 1914, USA: Wilshire Book Co., 1974.

Pedler, K. *The Quest for Gaia* UK: Granada Publishing Ltd, 1981.

Rees, A. & B. *Celtic Heritage: Ancient tradition in Ireland and Wales* USA: Thames & Hudson, 1961.

Ross, A. *Everyday Life of the Pagan Celts* London, UK: Transworld Ltd, 1970.

Shuttle, P. & Redgrove, P. *The Wise Wound: Menstruation and Everywoman* London, UK: Paladin Grafton Books, 1986.

Squire, C. *Celtic Myth and Legend* CA, 1905, USA: Newcastle Publishing Co. Reprint 1975.

Starhawk, *The Spiral Dance: A Rebirth of the Ancient Religion of the Great Goddess* San Francisco, USA: Harper & Row, 1979.

Stein, R. *Your Child's Numerology: A Means of understanding and developing their full potential* Richmond VIC., Australia: Greenhouse Publications, 1985.

Stevens, J.O. *Awareness: exploring, experimenting, experiencing* Utah, USA: Real People Press, 1971.

Stiskin, N. *The Looking-Glass God: Shinto, Yin-Yang, and a Cosmology for Today* Mass., USA: Autumn Press Inc., 1972.

Teish, L. *Jambalya: The Natural Woman's Book of Personal Charms and Practical Rituals* San Francisco, USA: Harper & Row, 1985.

Thorsson, E. *Runelore: A Handbook of Esoteric Runology* Maine, USA: Samuel Weiser Inc., 1987.

Valiente, D. *Witchcraft for Tomorrow* UK: Robert Hale Ltd, 1978.

Valiente, D. *Natural Magic* London, UK: Robert Hale Ltd, 1985.

Valiente, D. *An ABC of Witchcraft Past and Present* London, UK: Robert Hale Ltd, 1985.

Weinstein, M. *Positive Magic* BC, Canada: Phoenix Publishing Co., 1981.

Whitmont, E.C. *Return of the Goddess: Femininity, Aggression and the Modern Grail Quest* London, UK: Routledge & Kegan Paul, 1983.

Wilhelm, R. *The I Ching* Princeton, USA: Princeton University Press, 1967.

Zukave, G. *The Dancing Wu Li Masters: An Overview of the New Physics* NY, USA: Bantam Books, 1980.

Part V
APPENDICES

Appendix A
DREAMSTONE CASTING CLOTHS

Casting cloths marked with special patterns and divisions allow the diviner to allocate stones to particular times — of day, month and season. The corner designs are marked with the quarters of the moon, so that a stone which falls in that region of the casting cloth will have more significance to you during that moon phase. Similarly, the central design is marked with the four symbols for the solstice and equinox days, and the four cross-quarter days which are the peaks of the elemental and cosmic tides. This divides the year (and your casting cloth) into eight sections, radiating out from a central point.

Stones which fall closest to the centre of the cloth, within the circular design, are the most significant issues of a reading, and those which fall closest to the edge are peripheral matters or, as we discussed in *Interpreting the Oracle*, matters which are being ignored or avoided at the time of the stonecasting.

It is by no means necessary to have a cloth marked with these divisions, nor is it essential to use these divisions when interpreting the fall of stones — you can as easily use the bare ground or a plain cloth for casting your stones. I have come to appreciate the marked casting cloth, however, as it gives me the option of making two kinds of interpretation — the first concentrating on the pattern and relationship of the stones, and the second focusing on the development of matters over a period of time.

SYMBOLS AND DIVISIONS

The traditional divisions for a northern hemisphere casting cloth are:

NORTH	WINTER	MIDNIGHT
EAST	SPRING	DAWN

| SOUTH | SUMMER | MIDDAY |
| WEST | AUTUMN | TWILIGHT |

and the most common ones for the southern hemisphere are:

EAST	SPRING	DAWN
NORTH	SUMMER	MIDDAY
WEST	AUTUMN	TWILIGHT
SOUTH	WINTER	MIDNIGHT

The following casting cloth is divided in the manner described above, with the peaks of the elemental tides marked on the cross-quarter days.

A Dreamstone Casting Cloth

The approximate dates for the compass point divisions are:

SPRING EQUINOX: (north) *22 March* / (south) *22 September*
SUMMER SOLSTICE: (north) *22 June* / (south) *22 December*
AUTUMN EQUINOX: (north) *22 September* / (south) *22 March*
WINTER SOLSTICE: (north) *22 December* / (south) *22 June*

Peaks of the elemental tides fall on the cross-quarter days: *1 May, 2 August, 1 November* and *2 February* each year.

There are four quarters to the lunar month (marked on the corners of the casting cloth), each being approximately seven days long. A lunar month is approximately 29 days, 12 hours, 44 minutes long, so does not fit exactly into calendar months. There are thirteen lunations (lunar months) in a calendar year — a lunar or astrological calendar will provide further details on these cycles and will be available from most esoteric bookshops.

Appendix B
DREAMSTONE VARIATION: THE STONES OF BRISINGAMEN

by Bill Beattie

THE AESIR STONES

Odin

Of course, he is the real heavy of the Aesir clan, but, *Marvel* comics to the contrary, his primary persona is not that of an Icelandic Zeus/Jahweh/alpha plus male. As you'll remember from your planetary correspondences, he is one of the Mercurial Deities, rather than Jovian. More often than not he comes across through the Eddas and Sagas as very much in the Merlin/Gandalf mold. He's also the shaman par excellence of European mythology, a perpetual traveller in the deepest magics. In the stones, he represents magic (of the subtlest and secretest forms), shamanism, self-discipline, and the Questing Self. As such, he will be one of the major people to watch, indicating what's really going on, rather than what's footling about on the surface.

Frigg

The Goddess who launched some of the English language's most sadly abused words is, unsurprisingly, one associated with love, friendship, sexuality and harmony (Friday or Frigg's Day, in English, is Vendredi or Venus's day, in French. These linguistic correspondences work for most day names, by the by). Frigg is married to Odin but, unlike most of the Asynjur (Aesir Goddesses) who tended to be completely overshadowed by their mates (at least, in the Christian period literature), she retains a good deal of power. As a deity of love, she is the

168

principle of connection; through this she knows the future, 'all that is fated to be, Though she does not say so herself',[1] It is her power of connection we can focus on in a reading.

Thor

Again *Marvel* comics strike out. Thor (as revealed in slightly older sources) is less a Scandinavian Superman than an eccentric blend of Conan, Falstaff and one of those extremely large, furry, basically amiable but potentially volatile bikers you still see from time to time. Big, blustery (as his name reminds us, he is a Thunder God), somewhat dim — but the good news is that he's on our side. It is Thor, not Odin, who is the Jovian figure in this mythology. Odin was a God for Shamans, priests and madmen; Thor was the protector of the people. Apart from frequent rumbles with Jotun (a rival bike club across the water), he is more a defending warrior than an aggressive one. In a stonecasting, he will regularly appear as a clearer of ways, a supporter of projects or a protector against hostility.

Tyr

Tyr is more properly a Martial God; older, smarter and more level-headed than Thor (who took over from Tyr as the Sky God). Thor is the unthinking powers of natural energy working in our favour, whereas Tyr seems to manifest as a more human strength. Qualities of physical fitness, endurance, courage and will accompany his stone.

Baldr

'He is the best of them and everyone sings his praises . . . so fair of face and bright that a splendour radiates from him . . . the wisest of the gods, and the sweetest spoken, and the most merciful.'[2] Here comes the Sun, basically. And, like so many solar divinities, Baldr is also a slain and reborn God. His father, Odin, did the trick in a more overtly Christ-like way (hanging on a tree, pierced with a spear), but his sacrifice was purely shamanic, 'myself to myself', whereas Baldr's death is much more universally significant. As so perfect an example of the solar deity, Baldr will indicate all the traditional attributes of health, beauty, bounty and blessedness, with that death/rebirth twist dependant on how he is aspected by other stones.

Heimdall

If Odin embodies the mystical Mercurial qualities, Heimdall has cornered the market on awareness and communications. He is the Aesir's night (and day) watchman, guarding the rainbow bridge to Asgard. Nothing anywhere escapes his notice (except, on occasion, Loki who's rather good at that sort of thing). Heimdall's stone represents alertness, watchfulness and the ability to examine and evaluate situations.

Bragi

Though not a major figure in the mythos, Bragi earns a place through the value of his gifts to the world. 'He is famous ... most of all for eloquence and skill with words; he knows most about poetry, and from him poetry gets its name.'[3] By extension, he may, for the purposes of stonecasting, be seen to embody our artistic and creative selves.

Forseti

A particularly handy person to find well positioned in your reading, Baldr's son, Forseti, is a deity of judgement and resolution of conflict. 'Without exception, all who come to him with legal (or other) disputes go away reconciled.'[4] His could end up being your favourite stone.

Loki

And now for something completely different. Loki is sometimes considered the 'devil' of Nordic mythology. That seems a little harsh, particularly in view of the rather erratic moral dispositions of certain other major figures, including Odin himself. The mythology doesn't really accommodate simplistic concepts of good and evil. Loki is trouble though; disruptive, chaotic, anarchistic, iconoclastic — at best, a satirical humourist; at worst, a destructive cynic. His actions are often unforseeable, even by the likes of Odin and Frigg who specialise in knowing what's what. And so it is, in any form of divination, we must take into account that which will not reveal itself to us. In some myths, Loki is brother to Odin. In stonecasting, at any rate, he is of equal force.

THE VANIR STONES

Nerthus

I might be accused of cheating a little by including Nerthus among the Vanir, since she pre-dates the whole Aesir-Vanir mythos. She is, in fact, the primal Earth Mother, who comes to us by this name through a first century, c.e., account by Tacitus. As a chthonic deity of abundance, Nerthus seems more closely related to the fertility oriented Vanir than to the Aesir. In a casting, she will represent the old magic and deep mysteries of the Earth. Tacitus also mentions her associations with islands and lakes, with aquatic tendencies which link her more clearly to Binah and the Saturnian correspondences.

Njord

To the people of Iceland and Scandinavia, the sea was, and is, a major source of sustenance, and so Njord, God of the oceans and of mariners, enjoyed a healthy popularity. 'He controls the path of the wind, stills sea and fire, and is to be invoked for seafaring and fishing. He is so wealthy and prosperous that he is able to bestow abundance of land and property on those who call on him. . .'[5] And so, in a reading, he will indicate one's situation regarding travel (and attendant safety) and, perhaps, one's fortune on the choppy seas of commerce.

Freyja

Ah, my favourite. Like Frigg, with whom she is often confused, Freyja is associated with love, healing and with Odin. She is also a Goddess of Witchcraft (which she is said to have taught the Aesir), an aspect of which, combined with her attributions of fertility and graciousness, and her ability to be 'most readily invoked',[6] makes her a perfect patroness of practical magic. Although not explicitly linked to lunar imagery, her beauty and essential witchiness well qualify her to take on those correspondences.

Freyr

'He decides when the sun shall shine or the rain come down, and along with that the fruitfulness of the earth, and he is good to invoke for peace and plenty.'[7] If Freyja (Lady) is a Nordic Goddess of the Witches, her brother, Freyr (Lord), is the God. A Horned God without the horns — although his representations are often phallic (of the organic sort, as opposed to Thor's short but sturdy hammer). Freyr seems a particularly gentle fertility God, romantic as well as erotic, and his position in a reading will indicate the state of one's productivity in all areas of good works.

THE OTHER BRANCHES

Hel's Stone

Hel is a person as well as a place in Nordic mythology and neither are terribly nice. Hel is a place of the dead, generally the extremely dead (the livelier dead are taken by Freyja, Odin and his Valkyries). Unfortunately, there's not room here to look at the various places a dead Viking might have expected to have seen. Hel is a place where nothing ever happens; sometimes, a place of imprisonment. Hel, the person, is one of Loki's bizarre off-spring, 'half black, half flesh colour . . . she looks rather grim and gloomy'.[8] Although her two-toned nature seems to vary from story to story, her disposition doesn't. In a reading, Hel's stone represents entropy and stagnation.

The Norn's Stone

The three wyrd-sisters we all know (many also have peculiar brothers): Urd, Verdandi and Skuld (Past, Present and Future);

but 'There are, however, more Norns, those that come to every child that is born in order to shape its life.'[9] The Nordic concept of fate can sometimes bog down a bit with rather too much predestation. Basically though, The Norn's Stone will indicate those events or situations which we are pretty well stuck with, much as transit astrology will. Your own notions of fate or karma will inform you on how to read this stone.

The Elf Stone

Elves are ambiguous creatures in Nordic mythology, not necessarily either Tolkein's noble, spiritualised godlings or the egocentric manipulators of Poul Anderson's *The Broken Sword*. They are different to us, dangerously beautiful and essentially self-interested. However, I get on quite well with them and so, for me, the Elf Stone indicates luck, beauty and pleasure. If surrounded by enough dangerous stones, though, they may become Dark Elves. And then there are problems . . .

The Dwarf Stone

Dwarves know lots about the practicalities of life: about work, money, craftsmanship, money, self-reliance, money, manual skills, money and, of course, money. If they'd lost a bundle during the crash of '88, they'd have been out the next night, tunneling into the nearest bank. They are worldly; they are survivors; and, at times, they're damned useful. Don't overlook them in a reading.

The Jotun Stone

The rival bike gang again. Jotuns are giants, not necessarily hostile, not even invariably large (they seem quite handy at shape-shifting in some legends), but almost invariably they're in the way. The Jotun Stone indicates obstacles and challenges; surrounding stones will indicate the way over, around or through (or, if it's Thor's Stone, how to pound it to gravel).

FURTHER READING

Nordic Mythology
Crossley Holland, Kevin *The Norse Myths* Penguin, London, 1982.
Taylor, Paul & W.H. Auden *The Elder Edda* Faber & Faber, London, 1973.
Sturluson (trans. Jean I. Young) *The Prose Edda* University of California Press, Berkeley, Ca., 1954.

Seax Wicca

Buckland, Ray *The Tree* Samuel Weiser Inc., York Beach, Me. USA, 1974.
Adler, Margot *Drawing Down the Moon* Beacon Press, Boston, Ma. USA, 1986; for material on Odinism and other Nordic Magical traditions.

FOOTNOTES

1 The Elder Edda: Taylor & Auden translation, p.137.
2 The Prose Edda: Young translation, p.51.
3 'Bragr': old Icelandic for 'poetry'. Ibid, p.54.
4 Ibid, p.55.
5 Ibid, p.51.
6 Ibid, p.53.
7 Ibid, p.53.
8 Ibid, p 56.
9 Ibid, p 44.

ACKNOWLEDGEMENT

This article was reprinted with permission from the writer, and from *Shadowplay* where it first appeared in Volume 16, Winter 1988.

Appendix C
AFTERWORD: AN INNER JOURNEY

BEGINNINGS

Australia — an old land with an ancient spirit. Before the coming of the people of the North, the indigenous people of this land lived and worked their rites in harmony with the land. They knew how to find the places of sweet water beneath the earth, to hunt with the stealth of the wind in the grass, and to mark the Dreaming places with ochres drawn from the colours of the living earth. As a child of northern (Celtic) origins, growing up in modern Australia, I knew little of their ancient traditional ways, or the ways and lore of this land where I was born; but I grew into my own feelings and myths about the spirits of favourite places in the bush. The rocks, hills, rivers and the seaside have their own power and voice, which whispered to me in childhood dreams.

Before I learned that the Dreamtime is a mythic reality of the original people of Australia, I imagined it was a dream of the land and history; I had only heard the word, never experienced the context. I imagined that the Earth dreamed as we do; in flashes of colour, shape and meaning, and that these dreams became stones like opal and other precious gems. I remember being confused that jewels also came from other countries, which did not have a Dreamtime; however, in time I came to believe that all lands have their own Dreaming.

I imagined that if Earth-dreams were stones, then Sea-dreams were brightly coloured pebbles and shells, and the creatures of the Sea made homes from these shells and reefs of coral, just as humankind lived in the gift of the Earth — caves and hills made for us from the land. When I learned there was a series of Dreamtime stories and myths told by the Australian Aborigines (the Koori), I wondered how I could get the coloured stones to tell me their stories, imagining that they

175

would not speak a language I could understand.

I discovered mythology when I was told I was 'too old for fairytales'. My fantasy world became peopled by mythic figures from Australia, Greece, Rome, Egypt, Sumeria, Iceland and England. What a strange and colourful image of the world that mixture gave me! I read about Odin and his runes, of the Oracle at Delphi, of strange signs and portents which meant particular things to different peoples, and I became fascinated by the notion of secret glyphs and patterns. I remember gathering sticks and stones, colourful shells and pieces of sea-smoothed glass; carefully making patterns in the sand and throwing my motley assortment onto the spirals and circles I had drawn with a pointed stick. I stared at them intently, sure that they meant something, if only I could look at them the right way. I pretended I was the Oracle, a Witch, a Seer, Priestess or a god — games of a self-contained child with a rich fantasy life. The waves of the ocean would come and wash the patterns away, taking the stones back to the sea.

Sometimes I would make the patterns on the high tide mark to see how much was left after a few days, and at other times would create patterns of stones in small rock pools; building imaginary castles and labyrinths for crabs (cast as Theseus in my play) to disarray. These patterns and games faded into obscurity as time and the concerns of adolescence covered the myths of the maiden, until years later the search for spiritual understanding reawakened them from their slumber.

Tarot cards attracted me for a time, as they were very colourful and appealed to my imagination. However, a dream of stones lingered in the depths of my mind. Even though I 'knew' that stones were formed by stresses in the Earth on different minerals, I could not shake the earlier mythic certainty of their origin.

Personal myth remains a strong and binding force in determining the direction of my life and pursuits, and here, with stones, this is certainly the case. I am reminded of William Blake who said 'I must Create a System or be enslav'd by another Man's. I will not Reason and Compare: my business is to Create.'

The Dreamstone system provides a guide for you to explore your own interpretations of how energy works in your life, beginning with the simplest method of traditional lithomancy (stonecasting), using three stones and then developing the skills of that Art into the Dreamstone Oracle. This is divided into the Stone Pentacle — five stones representing Earth, Air, Fire, Water and Spirit — and the Three Rings, which consist of planetary stones and those representing Karma, Love, Life, Magic, Goddess, God and Random energy. The Three Rings were inspired by mention of a traditional divination system in Doreen Valiente's *Witchcraft for Tomorrow*. Through my own experiences and study of divination, I have explored this and other systems, such as sand and bone casting from Asia and Africa, corn casting from North America and Haiti, water, cloud and nature divination from Britain, Ireland and Australia. Elements of these other systems have been synthesised and incorporated into the Dreamstones, extending the traditional system of thirteen stones to one using twenty-three basic stones.

The resilience of the human psyche — to bend, shape and change reality, or to change the frame you use to interpret things in the world — together with the symbols from the Oracle and training in magical or psychological techniques (the exercises in this book are a beginning in this process), give you the ability to see where your own personal path leads. I hope you have found ideas in this book which will germinate your own personal system for interpretation of life's mysteries.

INDEX
Figures in italics indicate illustrations.